EAGLE SEAMANSHIP

EAGLE SEAMANSHIP

■

A Manual for Square-Rigger Sailing

Third Edition

Revised by Lt. Edwin H. Daniels, Jr., USCG

Naval Institute Press
Annapolis, Maryland

Third edition published in 1990.

Library of Congress Cataloging-in-Publication Data

Eagle seamanship: a manual for square-rigger sailing/revised by Edwin H. Daniels, Jr.—
3d ed.
p. cm.
"Published under the auspices of the United States Coast Guard Academy"—
T. p. verso.
ISBN 0-87021-251-6 (alk. paper)
1. Seamanship—Handbooks, manuals, etc.
2. Sailing—Handbooks, manuals, etc.
3. United States. Coast Guard—Officers' handbooks. 4. Eagle (Ship)—Handbooks, manuals. etc. I. Daniels, Edwin H.
VK541.E34 1990
623.88'226—dc20 89-13739

Published under the auspices of the
United States Coast Guard Academy

Printed in the United States of America on
acid-free paper ∞

9 8

Cover and frontispiece photographs:
Edwin H. Daniels, Jr.

Contents

Foreword

> The highest compliment one can pay a sailor is to call him a "Seaman." In that one word is expressed the whole mastery of his profession. Seamanship cannot be learned in a day, a week, or even a year, for within its meaning lies the ability to handle a vessel under any and every circumstance, fair weather or foul. Nor can it be learned solely from books. But as in every other profession, armed with the knowledge of what other men have found successful, the landsman in the light of his own experience will learn the more readily and surely.

This definition of seamanship is taken from the introduction to the 1898 edition of Luce's *Text-Book of Seamanship* (facsimile edition, Cornell Maritime Press, 1950), an earlier edition of which was used aboard the U.S. Revenue cutter *Dobbin* when that ship became the school of instruction for the first Coast Guard Academy cadets—the class of 1879. It is as true today as it was when it was written. Ships have changed dramatically since the days of the *Dobbin* of course; mechanically propelled vessels had begun to compete successfully with sail by the mid–nineteenth century (the Revenue Cutter Service built its first steamship in 1843), and by 1920 the age of sail was all but over.

But the sea has not changed. It remains the same unforgiving environment that it always was, as capable of destroying a modern supertanker as it was of destroying the frail wooden sailing craft of an earlier era. Anyone who aspires to become a seaman must begin by acquiring a firsthand acquaintance with the relentless forces of wind and wave at sea. Only by starting with such an understanding can the sailor learn to recognize and respect both personal limits and those of the ship on which he or she must depend both for survival and the successful accomplishment of assigned missions. It is for this reason—among others—that the Coast Guard, along with the naval and merchant services of many other nations, has continued to employ a sailing school ship to train its future officers. It has long been recognized that even in an age of technological complexity, sail training still provides the best possible foundation for seamanship.

Yet *Eagle* is more than a school for seamanship. She also provides an unparalleled opportunity for aspiring seagoing officers to develop confidence, courage, and good judgment: precisely the qualities the Coast Guard needs in its leaders. If wind is the force that can drive the ship, it is human ingenuity that has developed the means to harness that force, and it is the crew who must employ those means to make it happen. In *Eagle*, cadets *are* the crew. To sail the ship they must learn to work together as a team, to be decisive in circumstances that can be both frightening and physically demanding, to give and respond to commands quickly and clearly. And in the end, there can be few experiences as intensely satisfying as the successful accomplishment of a sailing evolution.

Eagle Seamanship is not a textbook. Rather, as the subtitle implies, it is a manual; and like most manuals, it is a descriptive guide to the use of a piece of "equipment"—a square-rigged sailing ship. If you are, like most readers, about to embark in *Eagle* for a training cruise, then it is important that you read this manual before you report on board; but it is even more important that you keep it in hand as you go about the ship to "learn the ropes," and that you continue to study it as the voyage, and your experience and understanding, progress. Here are distilled not only the knowledge and experience gained by *Eagle*'s sailors during her more than forty years of Coast Guard service but centuries-old traditions of seamanship as well. Few people have the opportunity that you have; make the most of it!

David V. V. Wood
Captain, U.S. Coast Guard
Commanding Officer

Acknowledgments

This new edition of *Eagle Seamanship* is the result of the efforts of many individuals. Almost forty years ago, the professional studies staff of the Coast Guard Academy locally produced a seamanship manual to help teach cadets how to sail *Eagle*. Although that first basic manual has been improved and revised many times, credit must go to those who first gathered information and organized it in an understandable form.

Eagle Seamanship was originally edited by William I. Norton, USCGR, and published in 1969. It was later revised by CAPT Paul M. Regan, USCG, in 1976 and was first published by the Naval Institute Press. The insights of then commanding officer RADM Paul A. Welling and sailing master CWO Richard T. (Red) Shannon played an important part in that edition. The history section was originally written by Robert Dixon, Jr., and was later revised and updated by Paul H. Johnson, head librarian, U.S. Coast Guard Academy. The work of all of these men has added immeasurably to the cadet training program and also forms the basic framework for this third edition.

Many of the changes in this edition should be credited to CAPT Ernst M. Cummings (commanding officer of *Eagle,* 1983–88), whom I had the privilege of sailing with for five years. His inspirational leadership and thorough knowledge of sailing and seamanship have taken *Eagle*'s training program to new heights and many of those improvements are reflected in thse pages.

Likewise, CAPT David V. V. Wood, *Eagle*'s

present commanding officer, has supported and played a vital role in this revision, as well as CDR Robert F. Petko, who initiated the project. In addition to that from numerous other good friends and shipmates, I received invaluable assistance and advice from LT Christine J. Quedens and LT Stephen P. How.

I would also like to thank the staff of the Naval Institute Press, who supported this revision from the beginning. In particular, Kelly Callaway and Marilyn Wilderson deserve special thanks for their untiring efforts to ensure that this edition is accurate and most useful to the cadet training program.

I personally owe any sailing abilities to my family, who taught me to sail and to have an appreciation for boats and the sea. *Eagle* primarily molds future leaders and gives cadets an appreciation for the challenges of the sea. It is that basic understanding of sailing and seamanship that has served Coast Guard officers well for years. My hope is that this new *Eagle Seamanship* will give cadets a basic understanding of square-rigger sailing that will help them gain the most from their hands-on *Eagle* experience.

Edwin H. Daniels, Jr.

EAGLE SEAMANSHIP

EAGLE HISTORY ▪ 1

Today's square-rigged barque *Eagle* is the seventh Coast Guard vessel to bear that name. The *Eagles* span many years and many changes.

The Coast Guard traces its history to ten revenue cutters authorized by the first Congress in 1790 at the instigation of Alexander Hamilton, the first secretary of the treasury. These ten cutters (so called for their English rig) operated as the Revenue Marine in collecting customs duties and enforcing the revenue laws.

The first *Eagle* was stationed in Savannah, Georgia, under the command of Captain John Howell. Howell's *Eagle* served as the Georgia cutter from 1792 until 1798 or 1799, when she was replaced by a captured French vessel and renamed the *Bee*. The United States had entered into an undeclared naval war with France in 1796. This war with the nation's former ally intensified when some sixty to eighty French privateers based at Guadeloupe in the West Indies continued to molest American ships. In May 1798, the United States Navy was formed to meet such threats and hastily acquired fifty-four vessels, of which eight were revenue cutters. This cooperation with the new navy established a custom that has been observed in all wars down through the years and remains in practice today.

The war with France was a strange war for it depended on sailing skill and bluff as much as on gunfire. Some fifty war vessels of the United States were divided into four squadrons, but the secretary of the navy, Benjamin Stoddert, insisted on a strategy where each vessel sailed an independent course. With some sixty to eighty French ships often chasing an equal number of American merchant ships and naval vessels, communications were sometimes extremely difficult. As a result prize vessels on both sides were often retaken. Though some ships never met the enemy, the relatively fast revenue cutters captured more than their share.

One of these valiant little cutters was a brig named *Eagle*. Designed by Josiah Fox and built in Philadelphia in 1798 by William and Abra Brown, the 187-ton vessel was 58 feet along her keel, 20 feet across her beam, with a 9-foot hold and a crew of seventy, including fourteen marines. She mounted fourteen 6-pounders through her gun ports.

The captain of this second *Eagle* was Hugh George Campbell of South Carolina, a demanding but efficient master of his ship. He was not afraid to challenge the secretary of the navy, who deemed *Eagle* ready for sea before he did. Secretary Stoddert ordered the ship to join the twenty-gun *Montezuma*, commanded by Captain Alexander Murray, and two other vessels in Norfolk. They were to cruise the West Indies to protect American merchantmen. *Montezuma*, however, sailed without *Eagle*. Piqued at Campbell's delay, Secretary Stoddert ordered him to cruise the coasts of Georgia and South Carolina. Campbell's later record in the West Indies raised the secretary's low opinion of him to such heights that in July 1799, Campbell was commissioned a navy master commandant. In October 1800, he was made a captain, which was at that time two grades higher than a captain of the Revenue Service.

In November 1800, Captain Campbell was selected to command the twenty-eight-gun frigate *General Greene* in place of Captain Christopher R. Perry, the father of the commodore, who had been relieved of his command for three months by court-martial. Captain Campbell was relieved in *Eagle* by Lieutenant M. Simmones Bunbury of Maryland. During the Barbary wars, Campbell was raised to the command of the frigates *Constellation* and *Constitution* and from 1805 to 1807 was commodore of the Mediterranean Squadron.

In the West Indies from 1798 to 1800, *Eagle* was one of the most successful ships, first in the squadron of Stephen Decatur, Sr., later in that of Commodore John Barry. In all, *Eagle* captured five French armed vessels. On two other occasions she assisted the ships *Delaware* and *Baltimore* in taking prizes. In addition, several American merchant vessels captured by the French were retaken by *Eagle*. One of her best captures was the schooner *Bon Pere,* which was renamed *Bee* and used by the American forces.

After Lieutenant Bunbury took command of *Eagle* at the end of December 1800, no further actions involving the cutter were recorded. The undeclared war with France was drawing to a close, and the new captain was told by Secretary Stoddert to "treat public and private armed vessels of France exactly as you find they treat American trading vessels." In a typical postwar economizing action—the war had cost the young government more than six million dollars—the second *Eagle* was sold in Baltimore in June 1801, for $10,600.

During the first two decades of United States independence, a diplomatic campaign was waged with England. Its purpose was to wrest from her a fair share of trade with continental Europe. Grievances increased in the early 1800s. American seamen, while ashore in British ports, were impressed into service on British ships. Since England was at war with France, she maintained her right to search neutral American ships and to seize what she considered to be contraband. It was intolerable, however, for Americans to be treated as colonists thirty years after the Revolution; President James Madison declared war on England on 18 June 1812.

During the first two years of the war, England was too busy with France to spare many ships for the American conflict. When Napoleon was exiled to Elba in the spring of 1814, however, the American coast was blockaded by the full power of the British navy. Revenue cutters, again cooperating with the United States Navy, did their share to protect the eastern seaboard and permit some coastal commerce. By the fall of 1814, several British ships had been captured, but two cutters had been lost to the enemy.

The third cutter to carry the name *Eagle* met the enemy bravely, but she too became a victim of the superior British forces. She was a relatively new schooner-rigged cutter, built in 1809 for the port of New Haven, Connecticut. She was armed with four 4-pounders and a pair of 2-pounders. She was commanded by Captain Frederick Lee, a noted Connecticut mariner who served as a state representative and founded Lee's Academy in Madison, Connecticut. In 1797, while a merchant captain, he brought the Polish revolutionary war hero, Thaddeus Kosciusko, back to the United States.

Eagle's job during the War of 1812 was to convoy American ships through Long Island Sound, since British men-of-war often entered the sound in pursuit of American merchant vessels. The sloop *Susan* of New Haven, under Captain Miles, was one of several packets that plied the sound between New Haven and New York. She was returning to her home port in October 1814, with sixteen passengers and a valuable cargo of flour, gunpowder, and dry goods, when she was captured by a tender from the British frigate *Pomone*.

Upon hearing of the incident, *Eagle*'s Captain Lee quickly recruited about thirty volunteers in New Haven to reinforce her crew and gave chase. An English 18-gun brig, *Dispatch*, accompanied by her armed tender and a sloop, chased *Eagle*. Light breezes prevented the cutter from out-maneuvering this far superior assembly of guns, so Captain Lee wisely headed for the Long Island shore and beached the cutter beneath a bluff at Negros Head. The crew dragged two of the 4-pounder guns and both of the 2-pounders up onto the bluff to defend their ship.

For six hours a battle raged. When the British were unable to drive the men off the bluff, they tried to destroy the cutter. The adamant men on the hill withstood repeated attacks, which continued through the night. When the wadding for their guns had been used, the crew tore apart the ship's log. They even picked up the enemy's shot from the ground and fired it back. Through it all, the American flag was kept flying, though on two occasions it required heroic acts to keep it so.

What was left of the cutter the next day was refloated by the New Haven volunteers, but *Ea-*

gle's worn crew could not keep her from the superior forces against them. The third *Eagle* was finally taken by the British.

After the war the Treasury Department commissioned William Doughty, a naval architect and constructor, to design three new classes of cutters to replace those lost during the war. Each design was modeled after the Baltimore clipper. The dimensions of the largest class were to be: 79 tons, 69 feet on deck, 19-foot beam, and a 7-foot depth of hold. The fourth and fifth cutters named *Eagle* were constructed from this design.

Little is known about these two cutters. Records show that the first was built in New York in 1816 and was intended for duty in Boston, although she was actually assigned to New Haven throughout her career. The second was probably built in Portsmouth, New Hampshire, in 1824 and stationed in New Haven until 1829. Both cutters were commanded by the same Frederick Lee who was skipper of the third *Eagle* during the War of 1812. While commanding the fourth *Eagle* in 1819, Captain Lee distinguished himself in a daring rescue off Montauk Point, a feat for which he received a handsome silver pitcher engraved with the details of the event. The careers of these two cutters most likely consisted of the routine duties of revenue cutters: insuring collection of customs duties, capturing contraband, and rescuing life and property endangered by storm or mishaps at sea.

Nearly a century passed before the Coast Guard revived the name *Eagle,* this time for a one-hundred-foot patrol boat. One of thirteen in her class, she was built at Bay City, Michigan, by

Defoe Boat and Motor Works and was commissioned 11 November 1925. This *Eagle* arrived at her assignment, New London, Connecticut, a month later. During the ensuing seven years there, she was engaged in enforcing an unpopular law: prohibition.

New London was the home of Base Four, one of the busiest operations in the Coast Guard's rum-chasing activities. An estimated one-third of all liquor smuggled into the country in the 1920s came from Rum Row, that notorious anchorage of supply ships just beyond the three-mile limit. The contact boats swarmed to these ships. The ever increasing fleet of Coast Guard craft was kept busy, picketing contact boats and an occasional brazen supply ship until contraband could be seized. Picketing and seizure comprised the duties of the sixth American *Eagle*.

This ship had a 210-ton displacement, a 23-foot beam and an 8-foot draft. She was equipped with two diesel engines, which drove her at 10 knots, not fast enough to catch many of the "rummies." Her armament was a single 3-inch, 23-caliber gun, which was sufficient to stop anything in her range.

A typical incident in *Eagle*'s rum-chasing career occurred in the late 1920s on a dark night, about forty miles south of Nantucket. The *Firelight,* a rum ship, or "black," as such ships were called, was already known to the Coast Guard. A year earlier her operators had been taken, convicted, and released by a typically lenient court. *Eagle* had taken over the trailing of the black from a destroyer, also stationed at Base Four.

The cutter started picketing *Firelight* at midnight. About twenty minutes later *Firelight* swerved, opened her engines, and came at *Eagle,* which was drifting nearby. The cutter quickly backed down to avoid the black, but her starboard side was struck lightly. No serious damage was done to the cutter, but the crew of *Firelight* had misjudged *Eagle*'s strength. *Firelight* began to sink, her underwater planking broken. The eight men aboard jumped into the water, where they were picked up by the destroyer and taken to New London to face charges.

In September 1932, the sixth *Eagle* was given a permanent change of station to Charleston, South Carolina. The duties assigned her were similar to those she had been performing in New London. The new presidential administration, however, soon ended the "noble experiment" of prohibition, and the following July other duties were found for the cutter at Charlotte, New York, and on the shores of Lake Ontario. A year later, the ten-year-old ship was sold.

The traditions of service developed by her predecessors are maintained in the seventh cutter bearing the name *Eagle*. Like her forebears and all Coast Guard cutters, the barque *Eagle* performs many missions. She has on numerous occasions been diverted to search and rescue and medical evacuations. In port, she supports the public relations program of the Coast Guard Academy, the Coast Guard, and the nation. During the nation's bicentennial, *Eagle* served as host ship for Operation Sail. Her primary mission, however, is to train cadets in seamanship under sail. This mission emphasizes the Coast Guard's firm belief in the value of sail training even in an age of gas turbines.

The training of cadets began in May 1877, aboard the topsail schooner *J. C. Dobbin*. Captain J. A. Henriques had two lieutenants and a few petty officers to assist him in instruction. The curriculum was composed of seamanship and navigation, and the ship sailed for five months each year between the United States and Bermuda. When she moored in New Bedford, Massachusetts, for the winter, academic subjects were added to the curriculum, and the first civilian professor was added to the staff.

The following year, *J. C. Dobbin* was replaced by the 106-foot barque *Chase*. New Bedford remained the home port of *Chase* from 1878 to 1890. After the suspension of "academy training," which lasted from 1890 to 1894, *Chase* moored for the winter in various southern ports until 1900, when winter quarters were established ashore at Arundel Cove, near Baltimore, Maryland.

Coming ashore did not mean giving up sail training. *Chase* served until 1907 as the Academy's training ship. European cruises, which had started in the 1880s, were continued. When *Chase* was converted into a barracks ship in Arundel Cove in 1907, she was replaced by a former Naval Academy practice ship, *Bancroft*, which the Coast Guard renamed *Itasca*.

The next cadet training ship was *Alexander Hamilton*, the third ship to be named after the founder of the Coast Guard. She had formerly been the naval gunboat *Vicksburg*, which saw service in China after her launching in 1898 and was later used as one of the state of Washington's naval militia practice vessels. She was turned over to the Coast Guard in 1921 and remained in service until 1930. Meanwhile, the Academy had moved from Arundel Cove to New London, Connecticut, situating first at historic Fort Trumbull in 1910 and moving to its present site in 1932. Until 1954, the mainmast from the cutter *Hamilton* served as the Academy's flagpole.

The Academy did not own a large training ship from 1930 until 1946, when it acquired the German training barque *Horst Wessel,* today's *Eagle*. During that period, sail training was carried out on a fleet of smaller craft: a two-masted Gloucester fishing schooner the *J. C. Dobbin II*, renamed *Chase*; a 65-foot schooner yacht, *Curlew;* the famous three-masted, 185-foot ocean racing schooner *Atlantic;* and a number of small yachts and dinghies. In these, cadets learned the rudiments of seamanship.

A most fortunate aid to Academy sail training occurred when the Danish full-rigged training ship *Danmark* was placed by her captain, Knud L. Hansen, at the disposal of the United States. This came as a result of Hitler's invasion of Denmark. From January 1942 to September 1945, officers and crew taught cadets to handle the 700-ton ship in every sea condition. *Danmark*'s mainmast still bears a bronze plaque commemorating her wartime service in the U.S. Coast Guard.

When World War II ended, the Danes said fond goodbyes, and the Academy looked for another training ship. Such a ship was found in Germany. After the war, there were three German barques to be shared by the Allied victors as war reparations: *Gorch Fock* went to the Soviet

Union, and was renamed *Tovarisch; Albert Leo Schlageter* went to Brazil but was later sold to Portugal and became *Sagres II,* and *Horst Wessel* went to the United States and became the seventh *Eagle.*

Mircea, a Rumanian vessel, is a fourth sister ship, also built in Germany. The fifth sister is *Gorch Fock II,* built by the Germans in 1958 using the plan of *Horst Wessel.* Some of the rigging used to build *Gorch Fock II* came from another training barque, *Herbert Norkus,* which was never completed because of World War II. The last time all five sisters were together was in 1976 in New York City.

The seventh *Eagle,* a 1,816-ton, 295-foot barque, was built in Hamburg in 1936 by Blohm and Voss. Named *Horst Wessel* after an early lieutenant of Hitler's, she served the German navy for ten years as a training ship, making cruises to the Canary Islands and West Indies. During World War II, she operated in the Baltic Sea, sometimes transporting supplies to and refugees from East Prussia. Her log records that she fired at Allied planes at least once, and that Hitler's birthday was dutifully observed on board.

In January 1946, Commander Gordon McGowan, who had been teaching seamanship to cadets, was ordered to head a group of ten officers and Coast Guardsmen as the nucleus of a crew to sail *Eagle* to the Academy from Bremerhaven, Germany.

Refitting the ship for sea in war-torn Germany took five months, and German sailors were then recruited to supplement the Coast Guard crew.

The return trip was made in June and July, by the triangular Madeira–Bermuda–New York route, along which the inexperienced crew sailed into a hurricane. But the seventh *Eagle* dispelled any doubts the skipper might have had about her seaworthiness. Although he brought his ship into New York Harbor with unseamanlike shreds of sail draped over her spars, the ship and crew arrived safely.

When the Coast Guard took over this *Eagle* in Bremerhaven, the figurehead was a handsome carved eagle. Its talons held a wreath, with a swastika inside, the symbol of the Nazis. The eagle remained but the swastika was replaced by the shield of the United States Coast Guard. The original figurehead deteriorated and has been replaced several times. The current figurehead was fabricated in 1977 of mahogany with a stainless steel rod, ensuring a longevity equal to that of *Eagle*.

Each year since 1948, *Eagle* has been the backbone of the Academy's summer professional training program. Accompanied by modern cutters, or alone, she has sailed the entire North Atlantic and visited almost every major port in Europe, on the East Coast, and in the Caribbean. On occasion she has sailed through the Panama Canal to the West Coast and in 1987–88 she made her longest voyage, a 30,000-mile round trip visit to the South Pacific and Australia to celebrate the Australian bicentennial. Whenever her schedule has permitted, she has participated in Sail Training Association races, competing against other "tall ships" from Europe, South America, and even Asia. On the Fourth of July in

1976, *Eagle*, as host vessel, led the parade of tall ships into New York Harbor for Operation Sail '76 to celebrate the United States bicentennial. In 1986, "America's Tall Ship" was again proudly the host vessel for Operation Sail '86, sailing into New York Harbor for the centennial of the Statute of Liberty. This celebration coincided with *Eagle*'s fiftieth anniversary.

Some 165 cadets can be trained at a time in *Eagle*, about six times as many as in a more modern cutter. This is an economic advantage, of course, but the main reason for sail training is the intimate knowledge of sea and wind that a cadet acquires from *Eagle*. In addition, upperclass cadets on board gain experience in leadership essential to their performance as officers.

This philosophy of sail training is reflected in the U.S. Coast Guard Academy mission:

> *To graduate young men and women with sound bodies, stout hearts, and alert minds, with a liking for the sea and its lore, and with that high sense of honor, loyalty, and obedience which goes with trained initiative and leadership; well-grounded in seamanship, the sciences, and the amenities; and strong in the resolve to be worthy of the traditions of commissioned officers in the United States Coast Guard in the service of their country and humanity.*

That is the mission, too, of *Eagle*, a name engraved deeply in the traditions of the Coast Guard, traditions nearly as old as the United States.

2 ▪ COMPARTMENTATION AND STANDING RIGGING

To fully appreciate the beauty of *Eagle* and to understand the traditions of mastering the sea under sail, one must first learn the vessel, her rig, and the language of the sea. Many of the terms and commands described in the following paragraphs have deep roots in the lore of square-rigger sailors of the past. By using proper nautical terminology, commands can be given safely and will be correctly understood. Thus, it is important for cadets to quickly learn to describe the various parts of *Eagle* and the commands used in all evolutions. In the following chapters, important nautical terms have been italicized. The glossary contains definitions of many terms not defined in the text.

HULL CONSTRUCTION

Eagle is constructed of German steel, using the transverse framing system. The details of construction are very similar to American practices of the 1930s. When *Eagle* was built, the technique of full welding had not yet been developed. In general, the seams are riveted and the butts are welded. Fittings are generally bolted while strength members, such as knees and gussets, are welded to the frames. The plating is approximately $\frac{4}{10}$ of an inch thick.

There are two full-length steel decks, a platform deck below those, and a raised forecastle and poop deck. The weather decks have a 3-inch teak deck laid on top of steel. The second deck is constructed of ¼-inch steel covered with vinyl tile. The platform deck and the tank tops are steel.

The second deck is the damage control deck. There are eight watertight bulkheads that run from the bilges to the main deck. These bulkheads have watertight doors on the second and third decks.

Figures 1 and 2 show the various compartments in *Eagle*. The compartments are designated, in accordance with standard U.S. Navy practice, using three numbers and a letter. The first number indicates the deck on which the compartment is located. The main deck is 1, the second deck 2, and so forth. Decks above the main deck begin with *0;* thus, in *Eagle* the bridge is the 01 deck, the top of the pilothouse is the 02 deck, and so on. The second number of the compartment number indicates the frame nearest the forward end of the compartment. The final number indicates whether the compartment is to port or starboard. Compartments to starboard are designated by odd numbers; those to port have even numbers. Compartments that extend across the entire width of the ship are designated by *0*. The letter that follows the three numbers indicates the use of the compartment. For example, *L* is used for living spaces, *E* for engineering spaces, and *F* for fuel tanks. The compartment number of the main male cadet berthing area is *2-63-0-L*. This indicates that it is on the second deck, its forward bulkhead is at frame 63, it extends across the entire width of the vessel, and it is used as a living space.

Fig. 1. Damage control diagrams

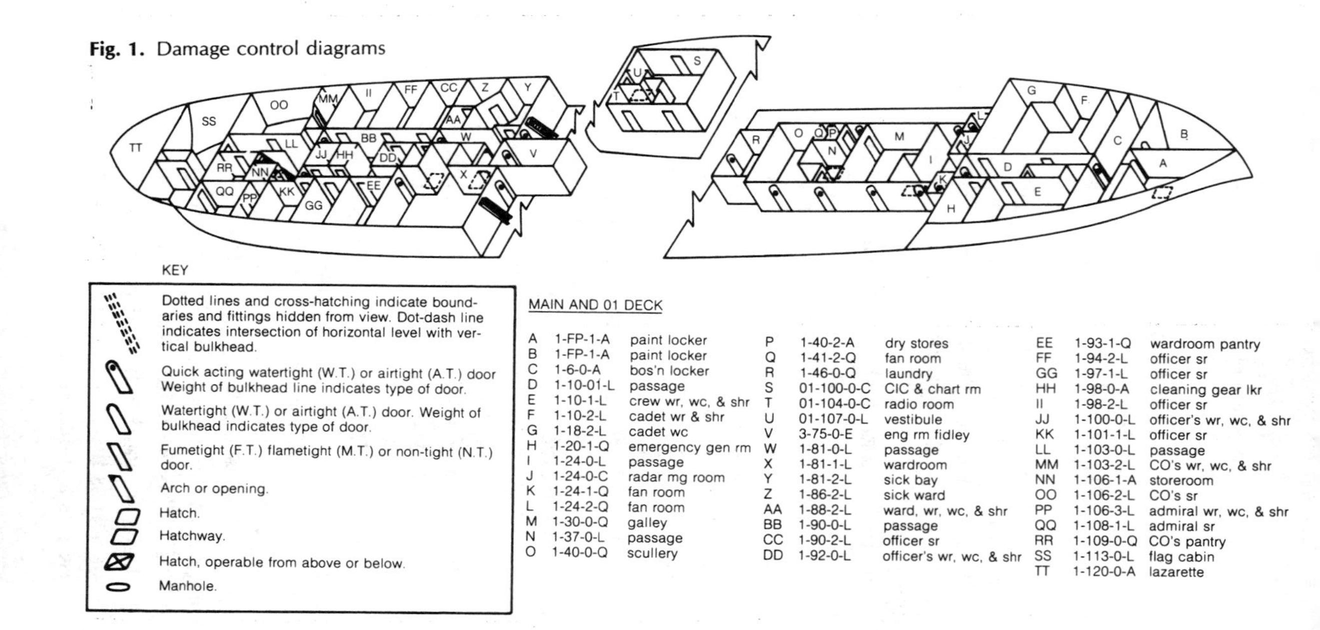

MAIN AND 01 DECK

A	1-FP-1-A	paint locker
B	1-FP-1-A	paint locker
C	1-6-0-A	bos'n locker
D	1-10-01-L	passage
E	1-10-1-L	crew wr, wc, & shr
F	1-10-2-L	cadet wr & shr
G	1-18-2-L	cadet wc
H	1-20-1-Q	emergency gen rm
I	1-24-0-L	passage
J	1-24-0-C	radar mg room
K	1-24-1-Q	fan room
L	1-24-2-Q	fan room
M	1-30-0-Q	galley
N	1-37-0-L	passage
O	1-40-0-Q	scullery
P	1-40-2-A	dry stores
Q	1-41-2-Q	fan room
R	1-46-0-Q	laundry
S	01-100-0-C	CIC & chart rm
T	01-104-0-C	radio room
U	01-107-0-L	vestibule
V	3-75-0-E	eng rm fidley
W	1-81-0-L	passage
X	1-81-1-L	wardroom
Y	1-81-2-L	sick bay
Z	1-86-2-L	sick ward
AA	1-88-2-L	ward, wr, wc, & shr
BB	1-90-0-L	passage
CC	1-90-2-L	officer sr
DD	1-92-0-L	officer's wr, wc, & shr
EE	1-93-1-Q	wardroom pantry
FF	1-94-2-L	officer sr
GG	1-97-1-L	officer sr
HH	1-98-0-A	cleaning gear lkr
II	1-98-2-L	officer sr
JJ	1-100-0-L	officer's wr, wc, & shr
KK	1-101-1-L	officer sr
LL	1-103-0-L	passage
MM	1-103-2-L	CO's wr, wc, & shr
NN	1-106-1-A	storeroom
OO	1-106-2-L	CO's sr
PP	1-106-3-L	admiral wr, wc, & shr
QQ	1-108-1-L	admiral sr
RR	1-109-0-Q	CO's pantry
SS	1-113-0-L	flag cabin
TT	1-120-0-A	lazarette

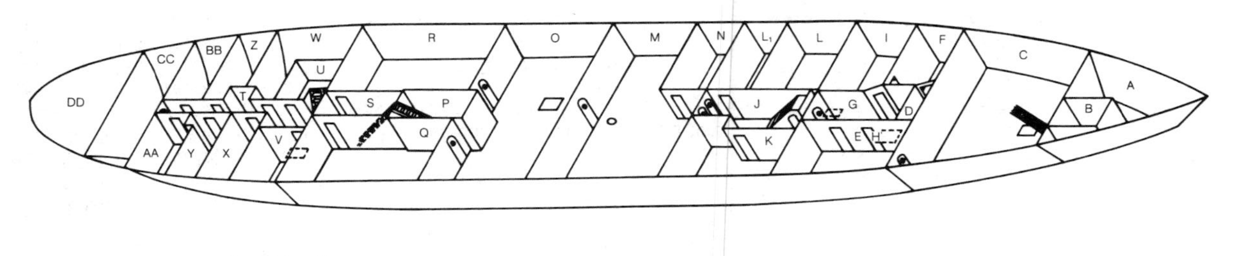

SECOND DECK

A	2-FP-0-A	deck store rm
B	2-6-0-Q	chain locker
C	2-10-0-L	crew's quarters
D	2-25-0-L	CPO, wr, wc, & shr
E	2-25-1-L	crew's lounge
F	2-25-2-L	CPO quarters
G	2-27-0-L	passage
H	2-27-1-A	cleaning gear lkr
I	2-31-2-L	CPO messroom
J	2-37-0-L	passage
K	2-37-1-L	cadet quarters, upperclass male
L	2-37-2-L	cadet quarters, upperclass female
L_1	2-41-2-L	first class petty officer berths
M	2-49-0-L	cadet messroom
N	2-49-2-L	cadet workroom
O	2-63-0-L	cadet quarters
P	3-74-0-E	eng rm fidley
Q	2-75-1-L	cadet quarters
R	2-75-2-L	cadet quarters
S	2-82-0-L	passage
T	2-90-1-L	passage
U	2-90-2-Q	eng log rm
V	2-90-3-L	officer wr, wc, & shr
W	2-90-4-L	XO's sr
X	2-95-1-L	officer sr
Y	2-99-1-L	officer sr
Z	2-99-2-L	officer sr
AA	2-103-1-L	officer sr
BB	2-103-2-L	officer sr
CC	2-107-0-Q	ship's office
DD	2-112-0-A	cabin stores

Fig. 2. Damage control diagrams

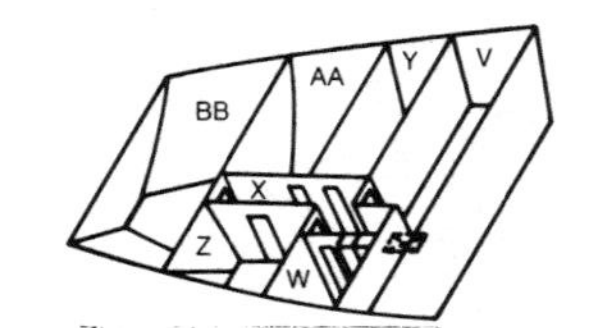

FIRST PLATFORM

A	3-10-1-L	passage
B	3-10-2-A	deck stores
C	3-16-1-A	cadet seabag lkr
D	3-17-2-A	crew seabag lkr
E	3-21-2-A	cadet seabag lkr
F	3-25-0-L	reefer flats
G	3-25-1-A	linen locker
H	3-25-3-A	stores room
I	3-29-2-A	meat room
J	3-31-0-A	vegetable box
K	3-31-1-A	dairy box
L	3-37-1-L	women cdt wr, wc & shr
M	3-37-2-L	women cadet quarters
N	3-39-0-L	passage
O	3-45-1-A	ship's store
P	3-49-1-Q	damage control shop
Q	3-49-2-Q	bos'n locker
R	3-56-0-A	sail locker
S	3-63-0-Q	machine shop
T	3-63-1-C	gyro room
U	3-63-3-Q	EM shop
V	3-90-0-Q	ET shop
W	3-93-1-A	movie locker
X	3-93-1-L	passage
Y	3-94-2-A	wardroom stores
Z	3-97-1-A	CMAA stores
AA	3-97-2-A	EM stores
BB	3-103-0-A	navigator stores

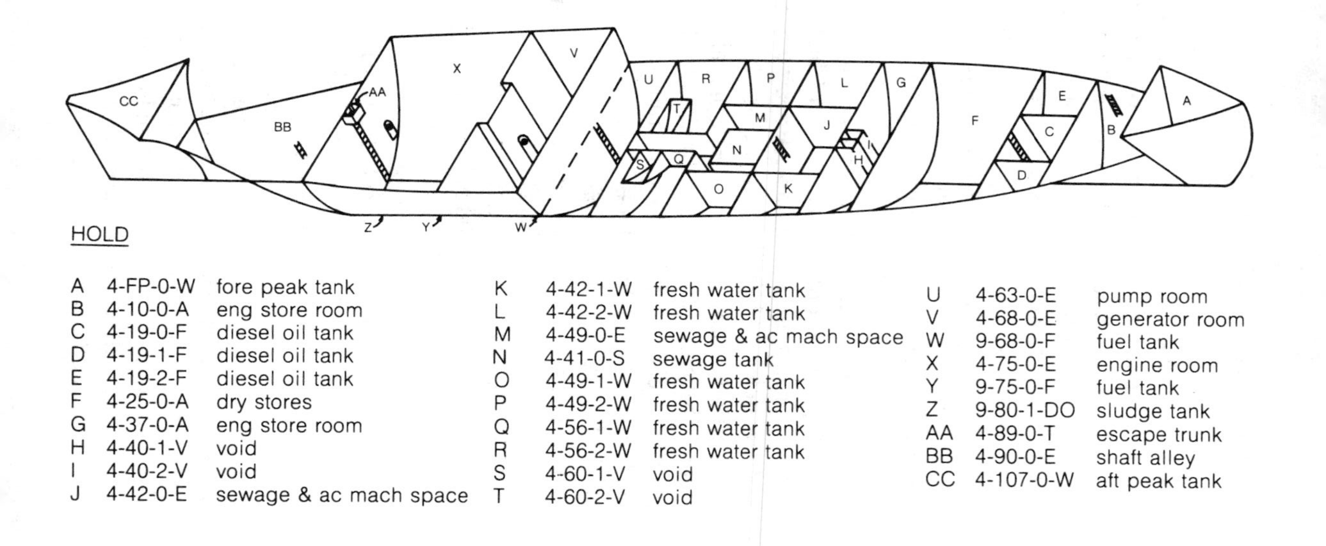

HOLD

A	4-FP-0-W	fore peak tank
B	4-10-0-A	eng store room
C	4-19-0-F	diesel oil tank
D	4-19-1-F	diesel oil tank
E	4-19-2-F	diesel oil tank
F	4-25-0-A	dry stores
G	4-37-0-A	eng store room
H	4-40-1-V	void
I	4-40-2-V	void
J	4-42-0-E	sewage & ac mach space
K	4-42-1-W	fresh water tank
L	4-42-2-W	fresh water tank
M	4-49-0-E	sewage & ac mach space
N	4-41-0-S	sewage tank
O	4-49-1-W	fresh water tank
P	4-49-2-W	fresh water tank
Q	4-56-1-W	fresh water tank
R	4-56-2-W	fresh water tank
S	4-60-1-V	void
T	4-60-2-V	void
U	4-63-0-E	pump room
V	4-68-0-E	generator room
W	9-68-0-F	fuel tank
X	4-75-0-E	engine room
Y	9-75-0-F	fuel tank
Z	9-80-1-DO	sludge tank
AA	4-89-0-T	escape trunk
BB	4-90-0-E	shaft alley
CC	4-107-0-W	aft peak tank

On the main deck of *Eagle* are the paint locker and the heads for the male cadets and crew. These are located below the fo'c'sle (forecastle) deck. Also in this area are the forward damage control locker, Repair II, (see *D*, passageway 1-10-01-L, on fig. 1) and the emergency generator. Aft of this are the galley, scullery, and laundry. The after section of the main deck, beneath the poop deck, contains officers' country and sick bay.

The second deck is the main living deck. The crew's quarters, crew's lounge, and Chief Petty Officers' mess are all forward. Upperclass male and female cadet berthing, First Class Petty Officer berthing, and the mess deck are all amidships. The mess deck is the dining area for the crew and cadets and serves as a classroom as well. The main male cadet berthing areas are aft of the mess deck. The after damage control locker (Repair III) is in the underclass male berthing area (2-75-2-L). The log office, additional officer staterooms, and the ship's office are located aft of cadet berthing.

The third deck, or first platform (fig. 2), contains the various workshops and storerooms needed to operate the vessel. Forward are the seabag lockers and reefer flats. Amidships below the mess deck are the sail locker, boatswain's locker, damage control shop, underclass female cadet berthing, and the women's head. Below the main male cadet berthing area are the machine and electrical shops and the gyro compass room. The lowest deck in *Eagle,* the hold (fig. 2), is devoted completely to fuel and water tanks, storage areas, and machinery spaces.

Although the number of compartments may be confusing, their location and use must be quickly learned. In an emergency, anyone may be called upon to assist damage control parties in any part of the vessel. It is also very important that all hands learn escape routes from every compartment in the vessel. These escape routes should be memorized and should become second nature, even in the dark.

MASTS AND SPARS

The lower masts, topmasts, topgallant masts, royal masts, bowsprit, yards, booms, and mizzen gaff of *Eagle* are all made of hollow steel tubes. All of these are known as spars. The foremast is stepped on the second deck, the mainmast is stepped on the keel, and the mizzenmast is stepped on the platform deck above shaft alley. The fore and mainmasts and their yards are identical. As shown in figures 3 and 4, *Eagle* follows the rigging practices of large sailing vessels in their final stage of development. The foremast and its topmast are actually one hollow tube, as are the mainmast and its topmast. They are rigged as the older vessels were, however: the shrouds come in under the tops, where a new system of topmast shrouds originates. The two parts of the mast retain their original names: foremast from the deck to the top, and fore topmast from the top to the crosstrees. The same applies to the mainmast. The topgallant and royal masts are combined into one hollow steel spar. The topgallant shrouds terminate about halfway up the spar. The portion above the topgallant shrouds is known as the royal mast. The follow-

Fig. 3. Standing rigging

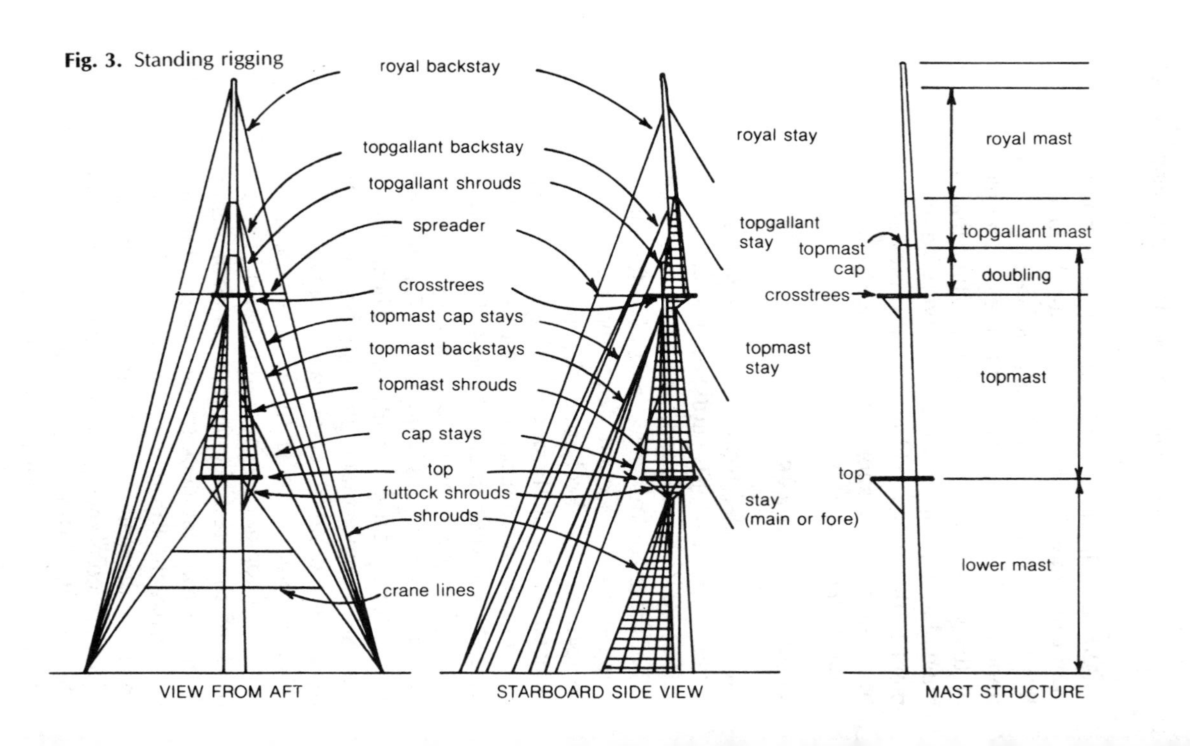

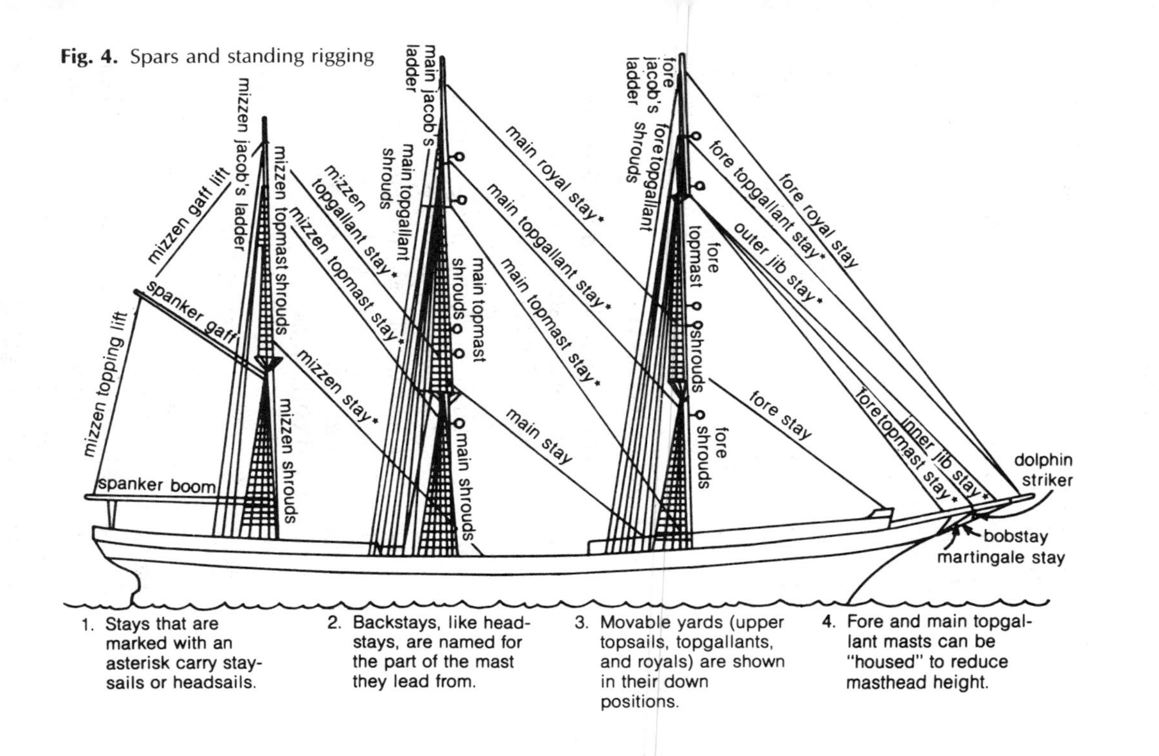

Fig. 4. Spars and standing rigging

ing table gives the names and weights of the individual spars:

Name of Spar	Length	Weight
Bowsprit	43 ft.	7,300 lbs.
Topgallant Masts	49 ft.	2,128 lbs.
Fore and Main Yards	79 ft.	6,380 lbs.
Lower Topsail Yards	72 ft.	4,840 lbs.
Upper Topsail Yards	63 ft.	3,520 lbs.
Topgallant Yards	50 ft.	1,700 lbs.
Royal Yards	38 ft.	884 lbs.
Mizzen Gaff	35 ft.	994 lbs.
Mizzen Boom	54 ft.	2,200 lbs.

STANDING RIGGING

In a sailing vessel there are two types of rigging: standing rigging, which supports the masts, and running rigging, which is used to *set, douse,* and *trim* the sails.

Since the standing rigging must support the masts against the tremendous force of the wind on the sails, it is made of high-strength wire rope. Standing rigging is not adjustable, and much of it is *wormed, parceled,* and *served* to protect it from rust and corrosion.

The three most important types of standing rigging are *stays, shrouds,* and *backstays* (see fig. 3).

1. **Stays** provide fore-and-aft support for the masts. They provide almost all of the support for the masts when the sails are aback (wind blowing on the forward rather than the after side). Since there are only a few stays for each mast, it is dangerous to be caught aback in high winds.

The *bobstay* of *Eagle* is a steel rod that runs from the bow, just above the waterline, to the *bowsprit*. The bobstay gives support to the bowsprit and allows it to take the strain of the stays that support the foremast.

As illustrated in figure 4, the stays are named for the part of the mast they lead to. The headsails and staysails are *bent* to these stays. In general, the staysails are named for the stay that they are bent to.

2. **Shrouds** provide athwartship support for the masts. *Eagle* has three sets of shrouds on the fore and mainmasts and two sets on the mizzenmast. The lower shrouds (see fig. 4) lead from the deck to the *tops* (lower platforms named for the "Fighting Tops," where marines were stationed in battle). The topmast shrouds lead from the tops to just below the crosstrees (the upper platform). The topgallant shrouds (mainmast and foremast) lead from the crosstrees to just below the *truck* (top of the mast).

Futtock shrouds are steel rods leading from the futtock band below the tops to the edge of the tops. They provide a foundation for the topmast shrouds and connect the topmast shrouds with the lower masts.

Ratlines are seized to the shrouds to form a "ladder" by which cadets may lay aloft. *Crane lines* are wire ropes that lead from the shrouds athwartships to the masts. They provide a footing for cadets handling the staysails.

3. **Backstays** provide diagonal support to the after side of the masts and provide the bulk of the support for the masts when under sail.

Other types of standing rigging include *foot-ropes*, which are wire ropes hung from *stirrups* under the yards to provide footing; *flemish horses*, which are loops of wire rope providing footing at the *yardarms*; and fixed *lifts*, which support the upper three yards when the sails are not set.

Principal Measurements of *Eagle*

Length overall	295 ft.
Length without bow-sprit	277 ft.
Length at waterline	233 ft.
Beam	39.1 ft.
Freeboard	9.1 ft.
Draft (fully loaded)	17.0 ft.
Displacement (fully loaded)	1,816 tons
Ballast (iron pigs)	344 tons
Fuel oil	24,215 gal.
Water	56,140 gal.
Height of fore truck (above waterline)	147.3 ft.
Height of main truck	147.3 ft.
Height of mizzen truck	132.0 ft.
Sail area	21,350 sq. ft.
Auxiliary power (Cater-pillar diesel)	1,000 HP
Speed under power	10.5 knots
Speed under sail	Up to 17 knots
Anchors (2) patent	3,500 lbs (port) 3,850 lbs (starboard)
Number of sails	22

SAILS AND RUNNING RIGGING ▪ 3

In a good breeze, *Eagle*'s twenty-two sails drive her faster than her auxiliary engine. The sails are set, doused, and trimmed using running rigging. The task of memorizing the location and use of more than 190 lines may at first seem overwhelming, but it is actually quite simple. The lines can be grouped into a handful of uses; their locations are logically determined by their functions. In addition, most lines are paired and located similarly on the fore and main masts. To understand these functions it is first necessary to examine *Eagle*'s sail plan (fig. 5).

SQUARE SAILS

Eagle has ten square sails. The sails on the foremast and mainmast are almost identical and are made of panels of dacron. The head of a square sail is attached to the *jackstay* on its yard with *robands*. *Earings* secure the upper corners of the sail using hooks on the jackstay to keep the head of the sail taut. The sides of a square sail are the *leeches*, the bottom is the *foot*, and the lower corners of the sail are the *clews* (see fig. 6). Running along the outer edges of the sail is a wide *tabling* of dacron, which helps shape the sail and give it strength.

Most of the running rigging is used to set and take in (douse) sail (figs. 6–8):

1. **Sheets** are lines attached to the clews and are used to haul the clews down to the yard below when setting sail. The section of sheet that

Fig. 5. Sail plan of USCGC *Eagle*

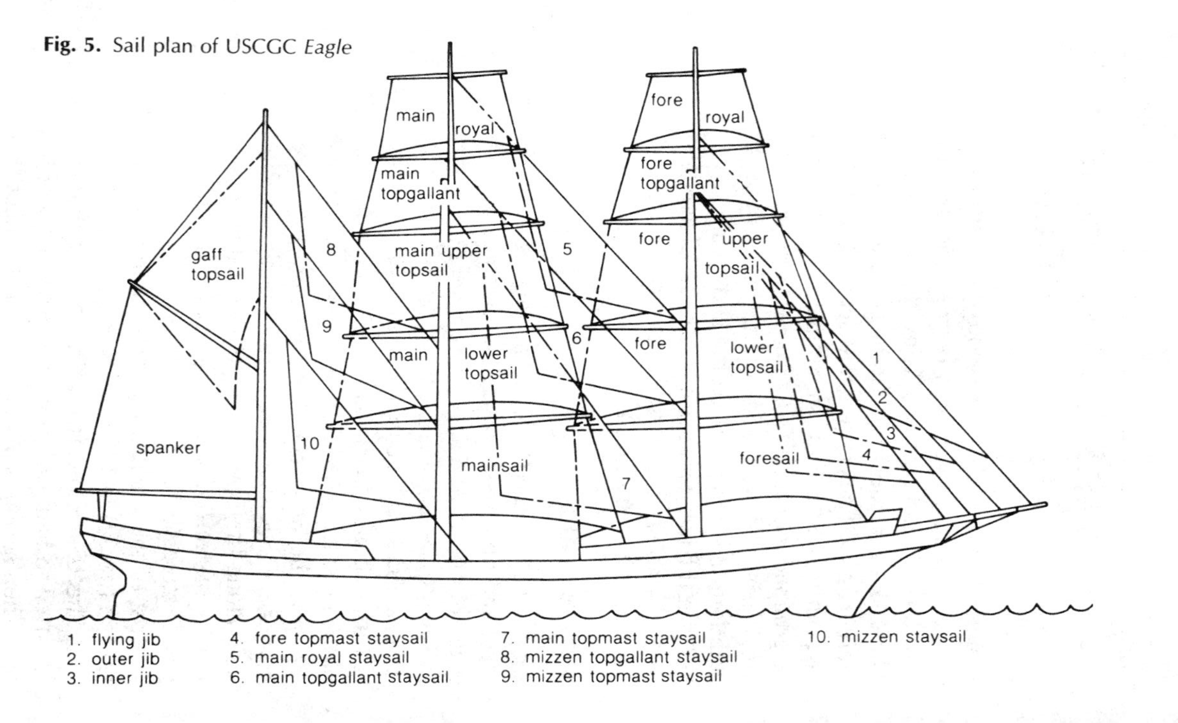

Fig. 6. Main upper topsail set

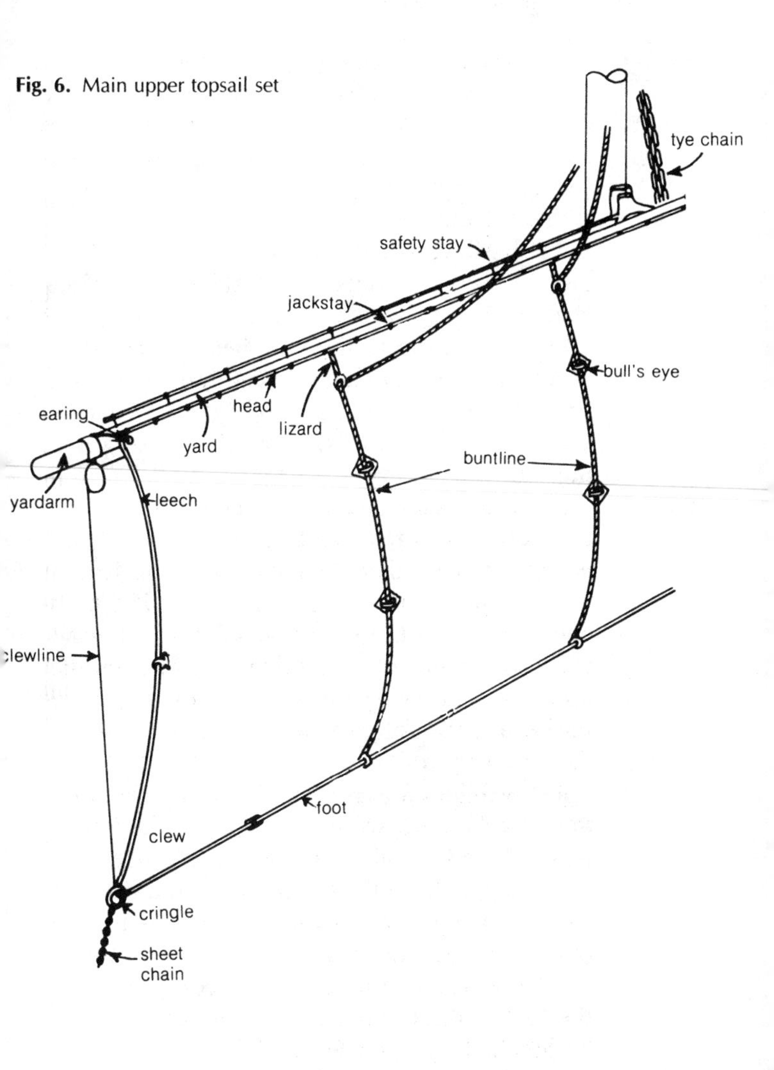

is led through the *cheek block* at the yardarm is made of chain to reduce chafing. The remainder of the sheet is wire rope with a single sheave block attached at the bitter end. All square sail sheets, except those on the *courses,* are belayed to the fife rails.

2. **Clewlines** are also attached to the clews of the sail but they oppose the sheets. Clewlines lead up to the yard on which the sail is bent rather than down to the yard below. Just as the sheets are used to haul the sail down when setting, the clewlines (*clew-garnet* on the courses) are used to haul the sail up when taking it in (fig. 7).

3. **Buntlines** are also used to take in sail. If just the clewlines were used, the sail would belly out in the wind so that it could not be furled. In heavy winds it would *luff* violently. The buntlines run from the foot of the sail through *bull's eyes*, which allow the buntlines to gather the sail up to the yard in several small bights. *Lizards* at the head of the sail provide *fairleads* for the buntlines (see fig. 8).

4. **Leechlines** are used on the courses because their leeches are so long that they are difficult to handle when taking in sail. These lines lead from the middle of the leeches up to the yard. On the topgallants and royals, the leechlines and outer buntlines are combined into a single *bunt-leechline*. The two functions are combined since the foot of these sails is short enough that it can be handled by a single buntline in combination with a bunt-leechline. The topsails do not have leechlines because their leeches are so short that they are handled with the buntlines and clewlines alone.

Fig. 7. Clewlines and sheets

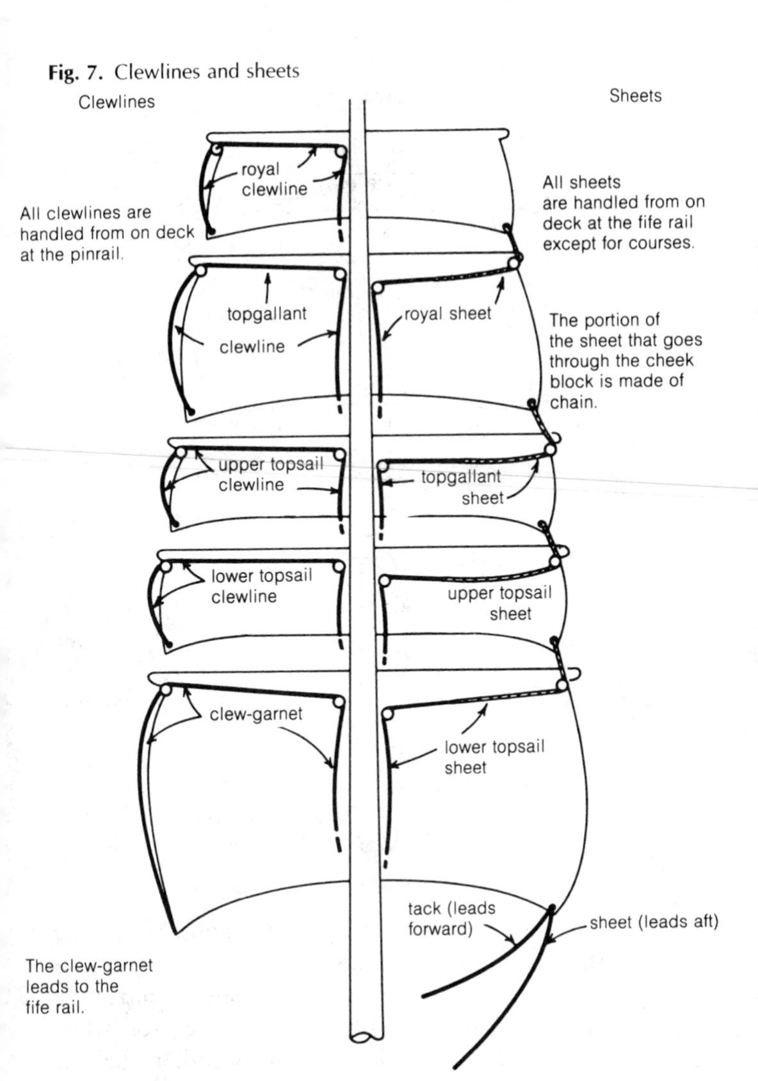

Fig. 8. Mainsail

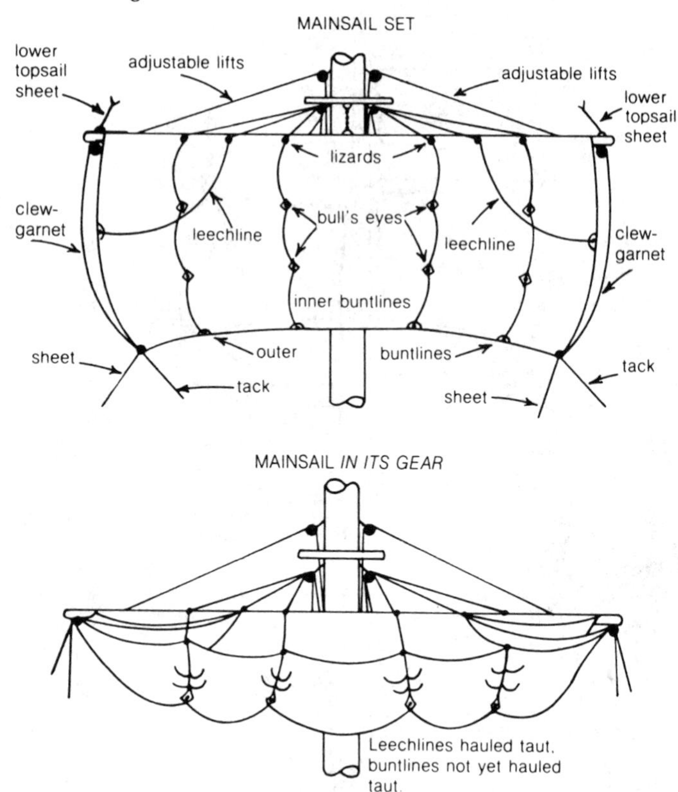

5. **Tacks** are used only on the courses. Unlike the upper sails, the courses are not set onto a lower yard. Thus, it is impossible to control the clew of the sail with a single line, for when braced sharp, the lead of the weather sheet is excessively long. (The weather sheet is the sheet on the weather/windward side of the ship.) Tacks serve the same function as sheets but lead for-

ward whereas the sheets lead aft. In setting the courses, the tacks and sheets are used to trim the sail and control the foot. When braced sharp, the weather leech of the sail is always flattened using a *tack-jigger,* a three-fold purchase attached to a pendant on the clew and to a padeye on deck (fig. 8).

6. **Halyards** are used to raise the upper three yards when setting sail. The upper three sails are set by hauling the sail down to the lower yard (*sheeting home*) and then hauling the yard up until the sail sets properly. The yards are movable for several reasons. First, having the yard down when the sail is not set lowers the center of gravity of the vessel and thus improves *Eagle*'s stability in a seaway. When a yard is *in its lifts* it is secure even in the roughest of sea conditions. It is also much easier to set and douse square sails with a movable yard. When a yard is in its fixed lifts, sheeting home is relatively easy since the sail will still spill most of the wind as the clews are hauled down to the yard below. The sail can then be fully set by hauling on a single line with a large mechanical advantage, the halyard, instead of two sheets whose mechanical advantage is much less.

Additionally, heavy weather or unexpected squalls often require taking in the upper square sails quickly. This can be done easily with a movable yard by easing the halyard and hauling the yard down with the clewlines. When the yard settles into its fixed lifts, most of the wind will be spilled making *clewing up* much easier. *Furling* is also safer since the yard is more secure in its fixed lifts.

HEADSAILS AND STAYSAILS

Eagle has six staysails and four headsails. Like the square sails, all staysails and headsails are made of dacron. The leading edge of the sail is the *luff*. Metal *hanks* are used to bend a sail to its stay. The lower edge is the *foot,* and the trailing edge is the *leech.* The uppermost point of the sail, to which the halyard is bent, is the *head;* the lowest point, to which the tack pendant is attached, is the *tack;* the clew is the remaining point, to which the sheet is attached. The edges of the sail, as with square sails, are reinforced with a *tabling* of dacron. *Eagle*'s headsails and staysails are scotch-cut. The panels of dacron parallel either the leech or the foot and are joined at the *miter seam*, which runs from the clew to the luff (fig. 9).

Three types of lines control the headsails and staysails: *halyards, sheets*, and *downhauls.* A tack pendant secures the tack to the mast on the staysails and to the bowsprit on the headsails. Used to keep the sail at the proper distance up the stay, it is permanently attached and not adjustable.

1. **Halyards** are bent to the head of a sail and are used to set a sail by hauling the head up the stay.

2. **Sheets,** as on square sails, are attached to the clew and are used for trimming. The headsails have two sheets each, one for each side, and thus their sheets can be shifted without dousing the sail. In contrast, the staysails have a single sheet that must be shifted from side to side. It is impractical to rig dual sheets for the staysails

Fig. 9. Headsail and staysail nomenclature

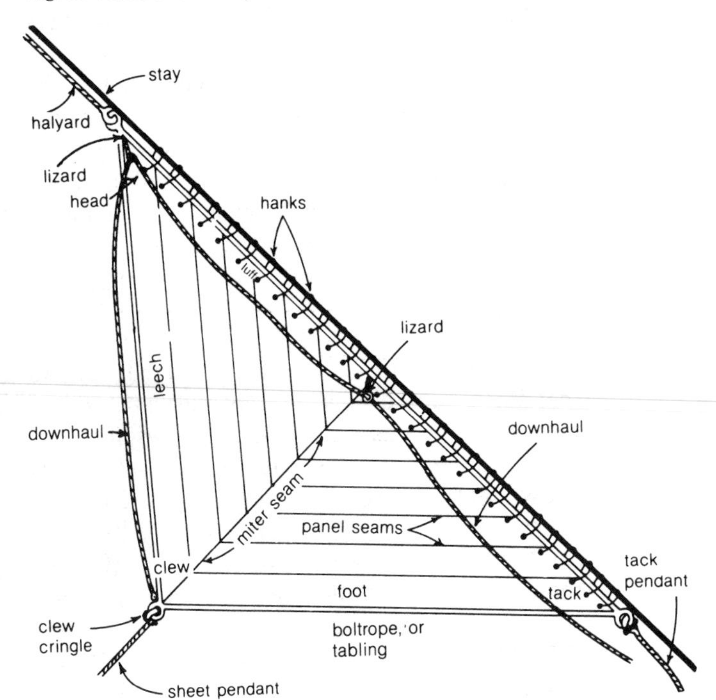

since they are set higher above the deck than the headsails; therefore, it would be difficult to haul the sheet over the lower stays from the deck.

The staysail sheets themselves are in two parts. A wire rope sheet pendant is permanently shackled to the clew of the sail. A sheet tackle is shackled to an eye on deck and to the pendant. In shifting the sheets, the shackle is unshackled and the pendant is hauled up and over any lower stays by cadets stationed in the tops. It is then reshackled into the tackle on the opposite side.

3. **Downhauls,** as the name implies, are used for hauling fore-and-aft sails down the stays when dousing. They lead from the clew through a lizard at the head of the sail and then down to the fife rail. This arrangement allows for better control of the sail when dousing. Hauling on the downhaul will raise the clew of the sail up to the head, causing it to spill its wind. Continuing to haul will pull the sail down the stay.

SPANKER

The spanker is rigged in a manner analogous to that of the square sails. The spanker's parts bear the same names as those of the square sails. Logically, the upper aft corner of the spanker is known as the *peak,* the upper forward corner is the *throat*. The lower forward corner is the tack, and the lower aft corner is the clew (fig. 10). The running rigging for the spanker is easily understood:

1. The **topping lift** is used to top (lift) the spanker boom high enough for the sail to set properly. When the spanker is not set, the boom is lowered into its cradle and secured with the spanker sheet.
2. **Outhauls** are like the sheets of the square sails and are used to haul the spanker out to the end of the boom and gaff.
3. **Inhauls** are like the clewlines of the square sails and oppose the outhauls. They are used to haul the head and foot of the spanker in to the mast when brailing in.
4. The **brails** are like the buntlines on the square sails and are used to control the body of

Fig. 10. Spanker

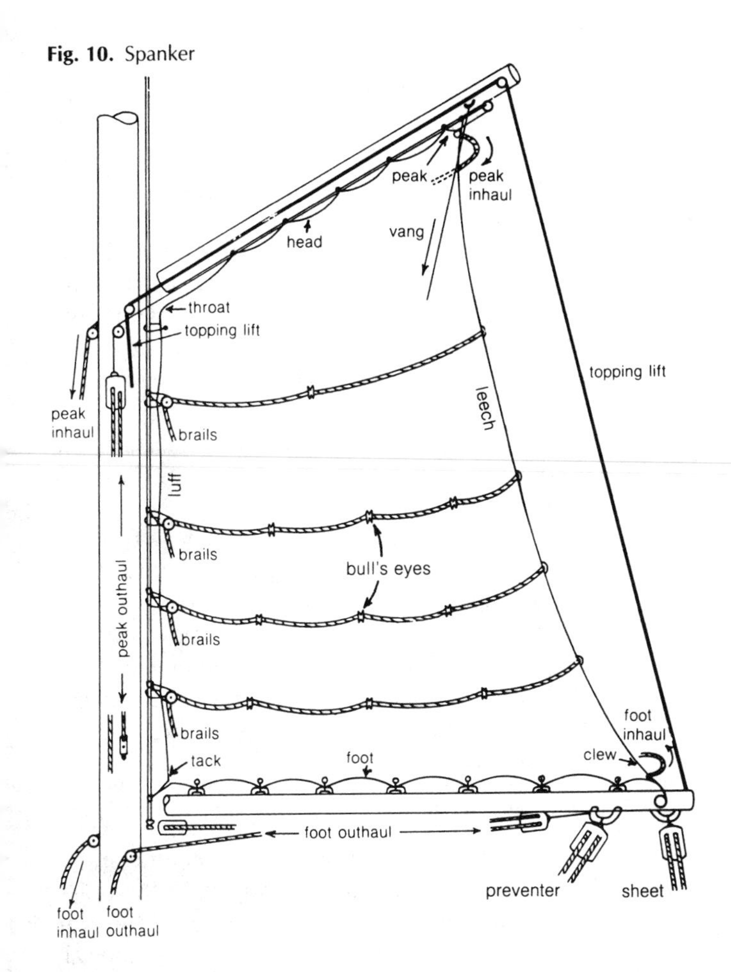

the spanker when dousing. Since the spanker can be set on either tack, brails are rigged on both sides of the sail.

5. The **spanker sheet** is a three-fold purchase that leads from *padeyes* on the fantail to the end

of the boom. It is used to control the spanker boom.

6. The **preventer** is a three-fold purchase used to oppose the sheet. Since the sheet leads from amidships on the fantail, it cannot control the swing of the boom. If *Eagle* gets caught aback and the boom starts to swing, the tremendous momentum developed by more than a ton of gear swinging out of control could easily tear the sail or even rip the boom from the mast. Thus, the *preventer* prevents uncontrolled *jibes*. Since only a single preventer is rigged, it must be shifted to the opposite side whenever the ship comes about. When the boom is cradled, it can be secured without the preventer by using just the spanker sheet.

7. **Vangs** are used to control the gaff. They prevent the gaff from slatting about (moving uncontrollably), particularly when the spanker is not set. When the spanker is set, the movement of the gaff is controlled by the spanker sheet, to which it is connected through the leech of the spanker. In such cases the vangs are used mainly for trimming.

GAFF TOPSAIL

The *gaff topsail*, like the spanker, is unique, although the lines function exactly as in the other twenty-one sails of *Eagle*. The parts of the gaff topsail bear the same names as those of a staysail (fig. 11).

1. The **halyard** is attached to the head of the sail and is used for setting (as with a staysail).

2. The **sheet** is attached to the clew of the sail and is used to haul the clew to the end of the gaff when setting.

Fig. 11. Gaff topsail

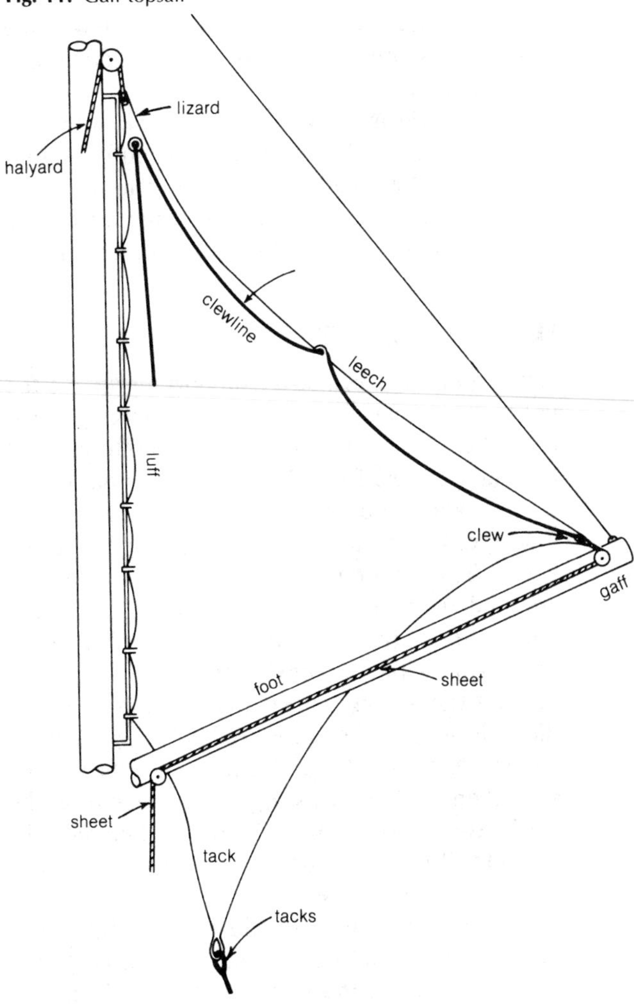

3. The **clewline,** like that of a square sail, opposes the sheet and is used to haul the clew of the sail in when dousing. It is also like the downhaul of a staysail.

4. The **tacks** are attached to the tack of the sail and are used to adjust the set of the luff and foot of the sail. Two tacks are rigged, one on either side of the gaff, so that the tack of the sail can be shifted to either side of the gaff without sending cadets aloft.

LIFTS AND BRACES

Lifts and braces primarily support and move the yards. The *timenoguy* is a special purchase, led from the mizzen shrouds, that is used to prevent the main braces from fouling on the boat davits when bracing the yards.

1. **Fixed lifts** are used to give support to the yards. The upper three yards are movable and are hauled up to set the sails. When the sails are not set, the yards settle *into their lifts*. These lifts are not adjustable. They support the yards and prevent them from working up and down. When the sails are set, the yards are hauled up the mast and the fixed lifts hang slack. The leeches of the sails then tie the yards together, preventing the yards from working up and down. When the sails are set, all of the yards can be trimmed at once with the main or fore lifts.

The lower topsail yards do not have lifts since they are fixed and do not have halyards. When sails are doused, the lower topsail yards can be controlled by the upper topsail sheets.

The *courses* have adjustable lifts. A lift pendant leads from the yardarms to the mast and then back to the deck via a three-fold purchase. The lifts are adjustable so that *cockbill* may be removed and the yards can be trimmed parallel to the horizon, the optimum position for sailing. As mentioned above, all of the yards are tied together when the sails are set, by the leeches of the sails. Sheets should be adjusted evenly on each side so that all five yards parallel each other and move together. Then, by adjusting the course lifts, all five yards will be trimmed simultaneously. The actual process of removing cockbill is described in chapter 5.

2. **Braces** adjust the fore-and-aft trim of the yards (fig. 12). The braces for the lower three yards lead directly to the yardarms from *bumpkins* on the sides of the vessel. The upper two yards have braces that are led from the mast astern and then to the yardarms. This arrangement results in a more horizontal lead and makes the topgallant and royal yards easier to control than the other three yards. All braces are paired. Whenever one brace is hauled, its pair on the opposite side must be eased.

LOCATION OF LINES

By now it should be evident that there are more than a dozen types of running rigging on board *Eagle*. Lines on deck are arranged logically so that it is easy to find any line once the location of a few key lines are learned. It is absolutely essential that everyone working the ship learn the lines since throwing off the wrong line can damage gear or seriously injure someone. For example, if the halyard for the upper topsail is thrown off by mistake, there is a good possibility that the top-

Fig. 12. Braces

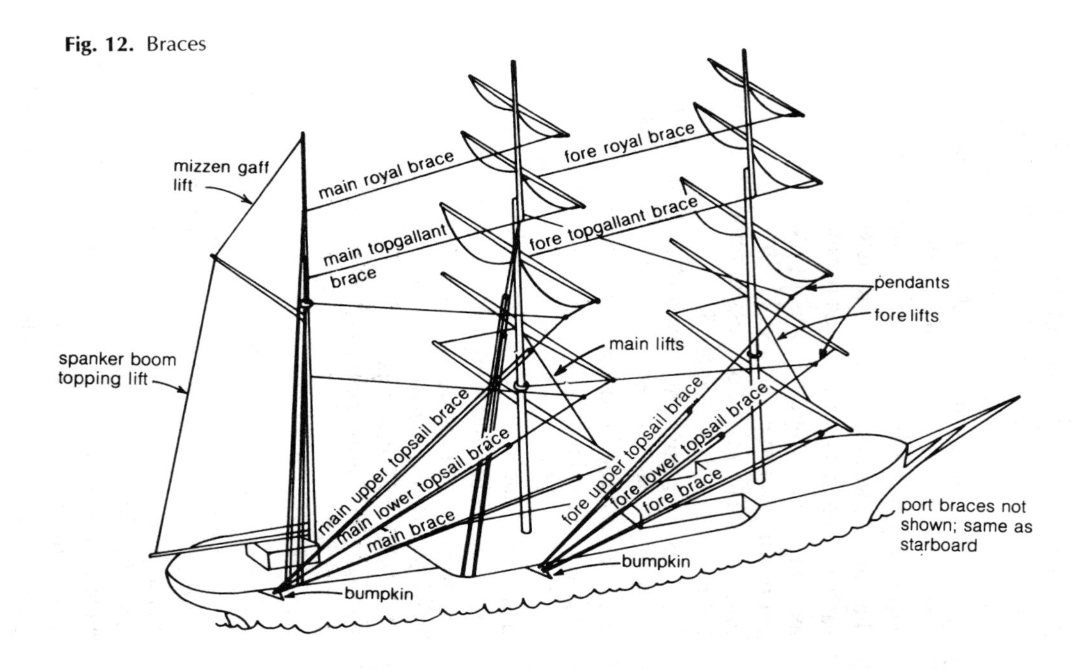

gallant square sail, which would have to bear the entire weight of the upper topsail yard and its gear, will tear. The tremendous weight of the yard as it slides down its track can also part the fixed lifts and result in the yard crashing to the deck. Obviously, safe operation on board *Eagle* depends on all hands knowing the location and function of the lines.

The general rule for lines is that the higher the sail, the farther aft the line will be located. Except for halyards, downhauls, and the lines for the spanker and the gaff topsail, all lines are paired and are positioned directly opposite each other on the pinrails and fife rails.

Clewlines, buntlines, and bunt-leechlines for all square sails except the courses are grouped by sail on the pinrails. The sheets for these sails are located on the fife rails. All foresail and mainsail lines, except the tacks and sheets, are also located on the fife rails. The fore and main lifts, which are three-fold tackles, are easy to identify. The clew-garnets are immediately forward of the lifts. The remaining lines for the courses are immediately aft of the lifts.

Staysail downhauls are located on the after side of the fife rails. Headsail downhauls are located forward on the dograil. Headsail sheets lead to the monkey rails on the fo'c'sle. The staysail sheets lead to the pinrails.

The halyards are grouped together. By locating the upper topsail halyard, it is easy to locate the remaining halyards on the fore and main. On both masts the upper topsail halyard has the largest line and the largest purchase. They are

Fig. 13. Pinrail, forecastle

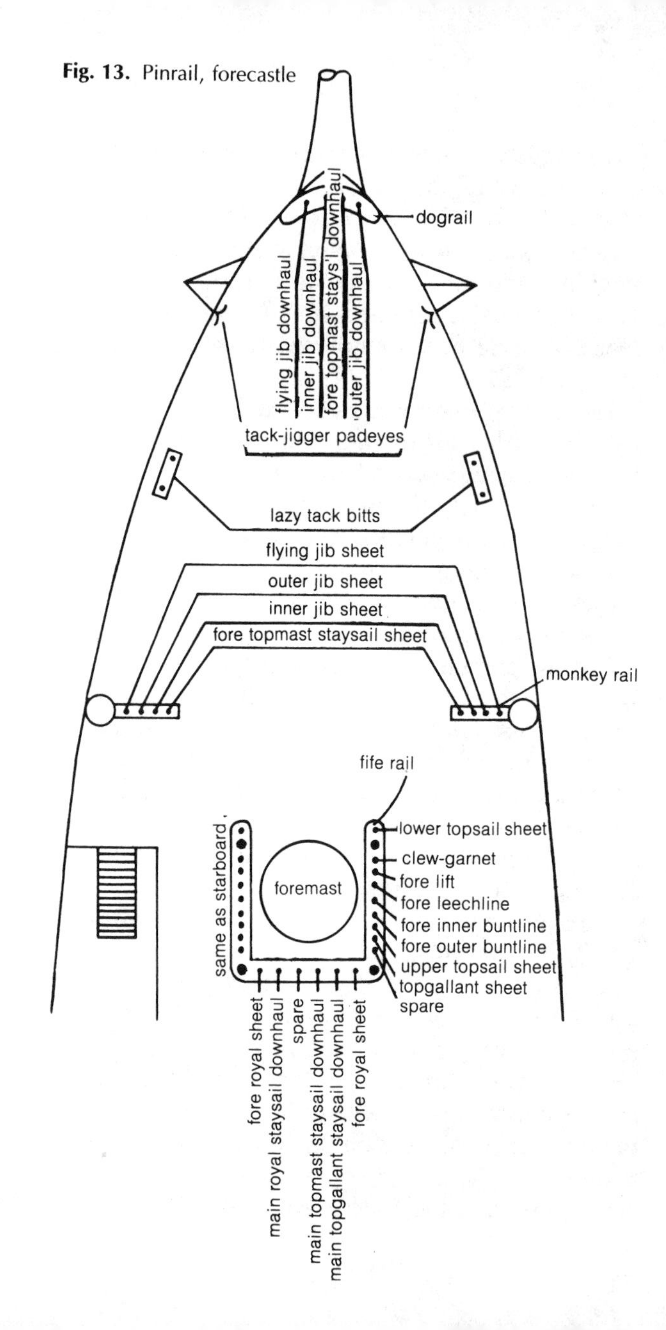

Fig. 14. Pinrail, waist forward

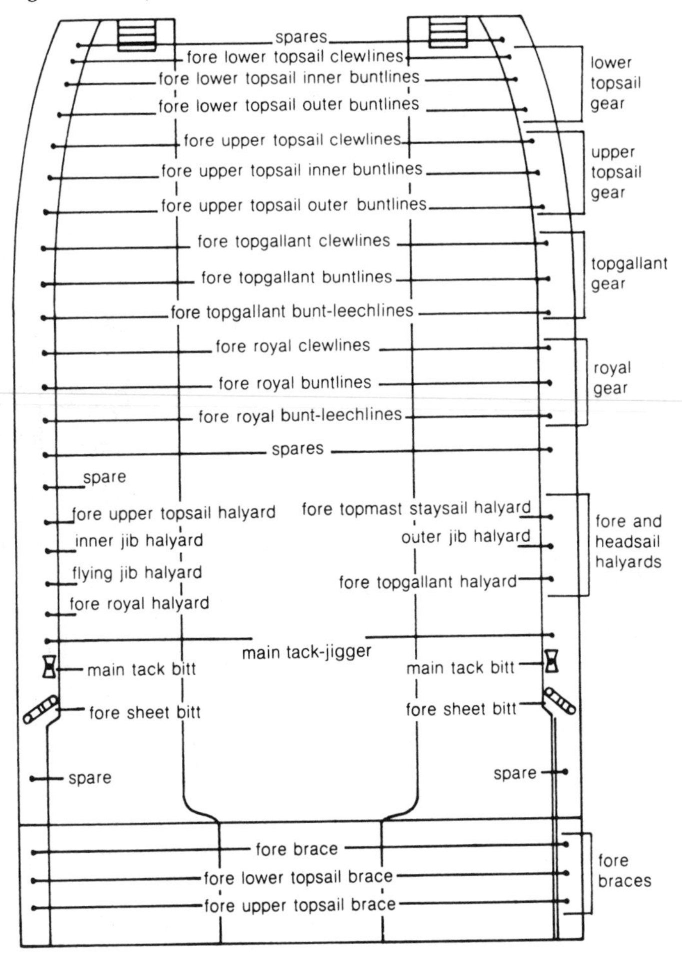

Fig. 15. Pinrails, waist aft

A. Pinrails

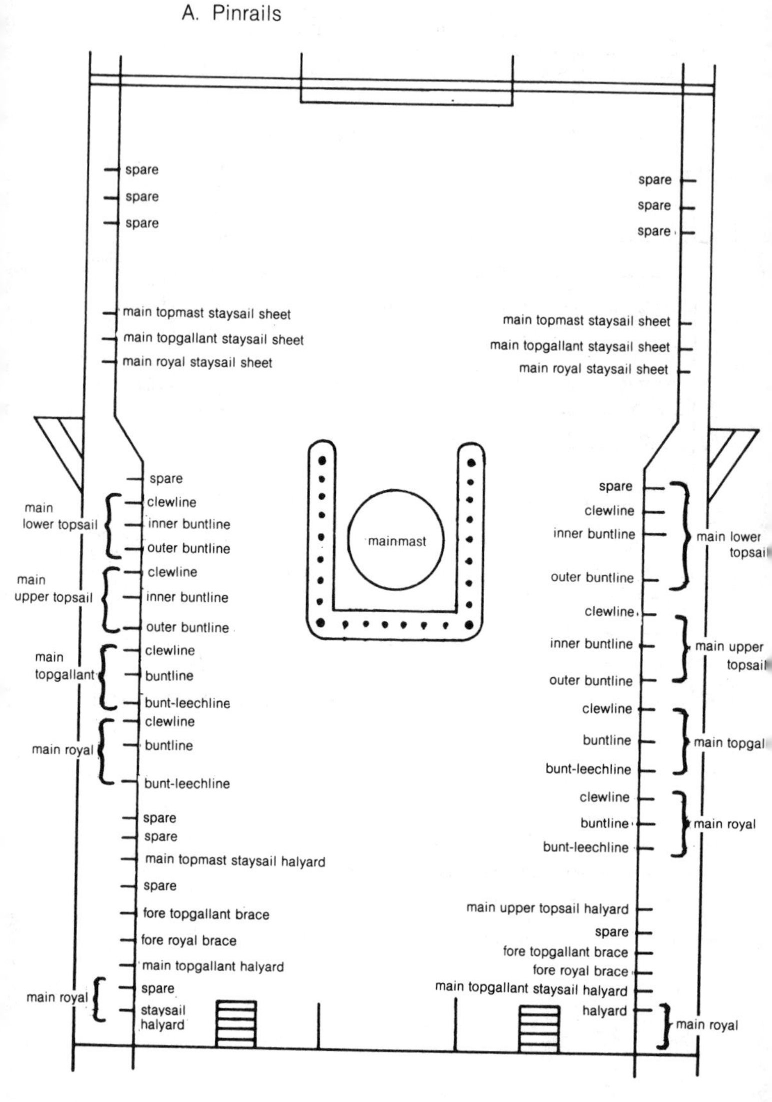

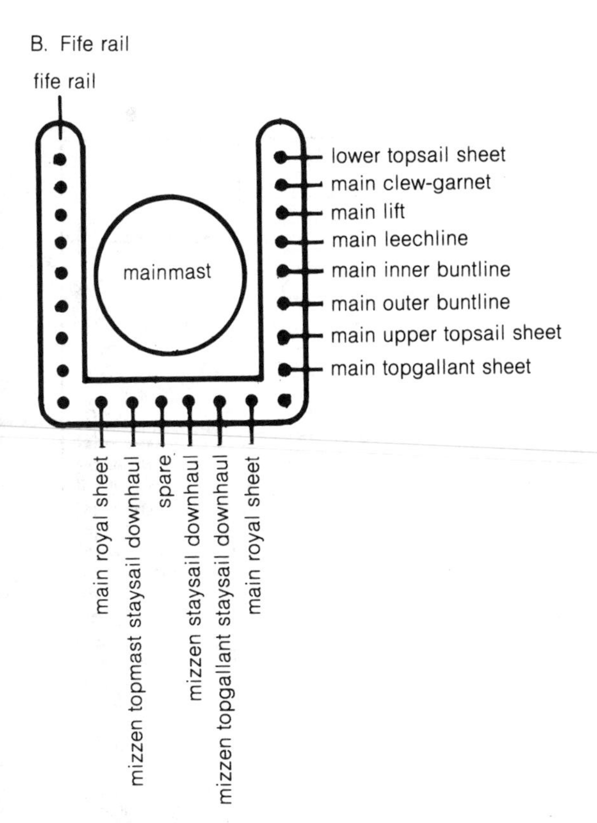

located on the port side on the fore and the starboard side on the main so that cadets setting the upper topsails will not interfere with each other when hauling on the halyards. The topgallant halyards are on the opposite pinrail, farther aft and with slightly smaller purchases. Finally, alternating again to the original side, are the royal halyards with the smallest purchases. They are farthest aft. Once the square sail halyards are learned, it is easy to locate the headsail and stay-

Fig. 16. Pinrails, mizzenmast

A. Pinrails

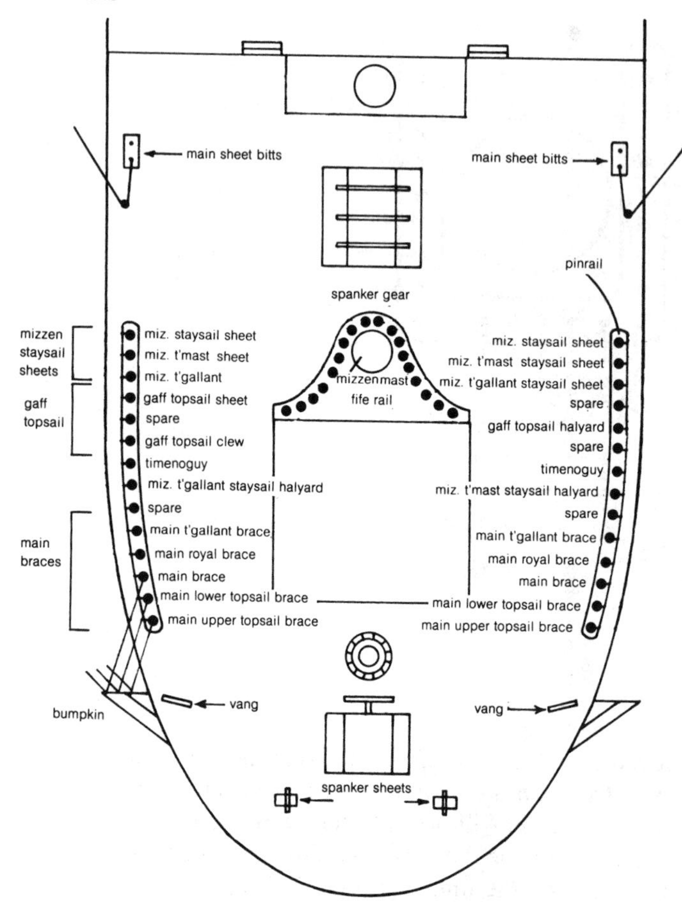

B. Fife rail

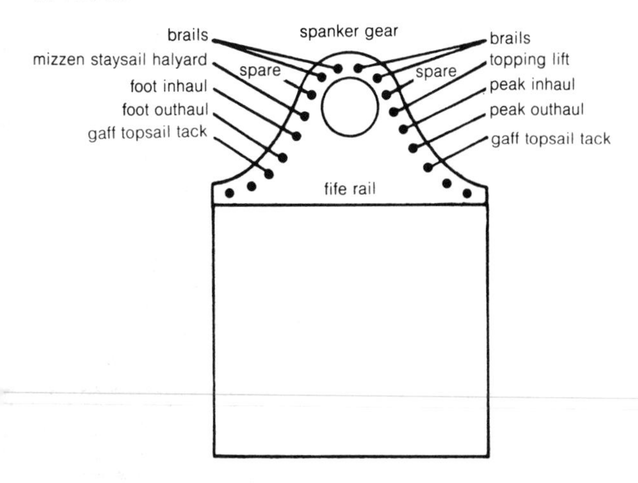

sail halyards. Directly opposite the upper topsail halyard are the topmast staysail halyards. Opposite, the main topgallant and royal halyards are the main topgallant staysail and royal staysail halyards, respectively. The headsail halyards alternate from starboard to port, the halyard to the higher sail being aft. Opposite, but slightly aft of the fore topmast staysail halyard, is the inner jib halyard. The outer jib halyard is immediately aft of the fore topmast staysail halyard. Finally, the flying jib is immediately aft of the inner jib halyard. The halyards for the mizzen staysails and gaff topsail are located on the mizzen pinrails, except for the mizzen staysail halyard, which is on the fife rail. Lines for the spanker except for the sheets are located on the mizzen fife rail.

The accompanying diagrams (figs. 13–17) should be studied to learn line locations. Lines

Fig. 17. Location of halyards

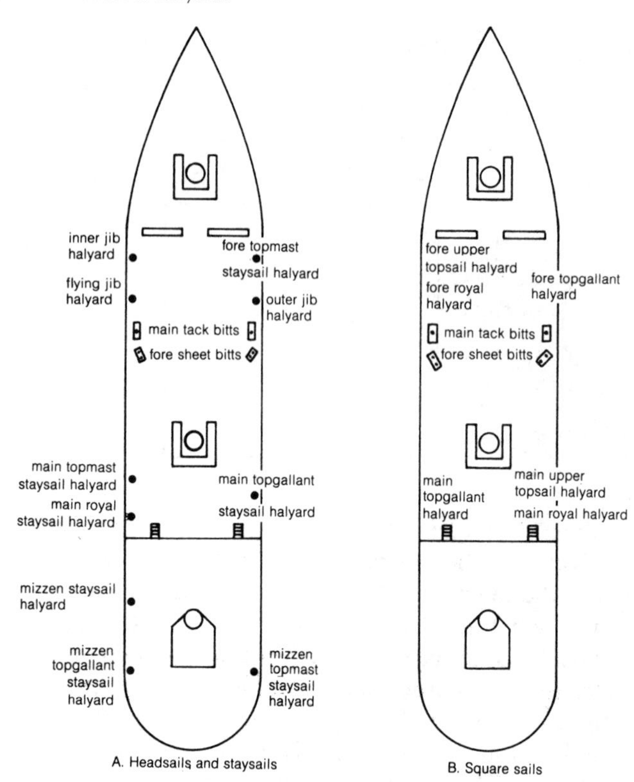

RULE: Staysail and headsail halyards alternate port and starboard. On the main and mizzen, only the halyard for the intermediate staysail is to starboard; halyards for the lowest and the highest staysails are to port.

RULE: Square sail halyards alternate port and starboard, aft and upward. For a quick reference, locate the largest purchase. It will be the upper topsail halyard. Royal will be a few pins aft on the same side with a smaller purchase. Topgallant will be on the other side with intermediate purchase. All square sail halyards are belayed to extra long pins.

can usually be identified by their size, lead, type, and position. For instance, all halyards have accompanying stoppers on deck to help belay them when under a strain. Again, if the functions of the lines are understood and the position of the most obvious lines memorized, it will be relatively easy to identify the remaining lines. To understand sailing *Eagle*, you must first learn the lines and their functions.

SETTING, DOUSING, AND FURLING SAIL ▪ 4

Sailing a square-rigger requires organization and teamwork to ensure that evolutions are safe and efficient. Because *Eagle* is a training vessel, this is particularly true. The failure of a single cadet to ease a line at the proper time can prevent the ship from tacking. Throwing off a line at the wrong time can injure or kill a shipmate. In no other setting is the need for and importance of a well-ordered chain of command so apparent. One of the most significant reasons for training on board a sailing ship is the opportunity cadets are given to organize and direct people into a close-knit team responsive to the orders of the Commanding Officer. If any part fails, a ten-minute operation can easily grow into an hour of hard labor. The consequences of failing to organize properly and the great importance of every cadet in the chain of command are reinforced by extra time and effort needed when an evolution fails. On the other hand, a well-prepared team will execute commands and evolutions easily and their teamwork and preparation will be readily apparent.

ORGANIZATION

Cadets fill all sailing billets from top to bottom in the chain of command. Each cadet in a supervisory position is supported by an officer or a petty officer who acts as the safety observer and technical advisor.

The chain of command for a sailing evolution starts with the Cadet Officer of the Deck, who acts as sailmaster under the direct supervision of the Officer of the Deck (OOD) and the Commanding Officer (CO). The Cadet OOD is responsible for the successful and safe completion of the evolution. The three Cadet Mast Captains, supported by the Mast Officers and Mast Petty Officers, report to the Cadet OOD. The Mast Captains must assign upperclass cadets to act as supervisors in key positions. These positions depend upon the evolution but generally include cadets in charge of each pinrail, fife rail, the braces, the headsails, and the staysails.

When problems arise, it is usually at this intermediate level of command. In most evolutions it is impossible for the mast captain to observe every line personally so supervisors must learn to delegate. Yet without proper supervision, a minor problem with one line can easily become a major problem for the entire mast. The use of upperclass supervisors reduces the mast captain's span of control to a more manageable four or five cadets and allows the mast captain to devote more time to the evolution as a whole. In general, these upperclass supervisors should remain at their stations throughout an evolution so they are always ready to respond to commands and direct the efforts of the underclass cadets.

Underclass cadets are an integral part of the chain of command, and are usually assigned to specific lines or yards. Pinrail and Fife Rail Captains assign cadets to specific lines. The Line Captain is responsible for ensuring that the line is fully ready before reporting "*Manned and ready*" to the supervisor. Specifically, the line captain must ensure that the line is properly faked out for running or led clear for hauling and that a sufficient number of cadets have manned the line to accomplish the task.

The number of cadets required usually depends upon wind and sea conditions, so the upperclass supervisor must intelligently gauge the conditions to assign the appropriate number of cadets. For example, assigning four or five cadets to ease a line with no strain on it is wasteful. Conversely, assigning one or two cadets to tend a staysail sheet in high winds can be very dangerous.

The remaining underclass cadets are also an essential part of the chain of command: the success or failure of the evolution often depends on the actions of these cadets. The underclass cadets must be well prepared and pay attention at all times so they do not miss a command or respond to the command given to another line or mast. Additionally, they must act as safety observers and report fouled lines and other problems to their supervisor. Having a thorough knowledge of the lines and commands is essential. Being well prepared will make all evolutions safer and make them easier to understand. It is important for the underclass cadets to learn all that they can since someday they will be in a supervisory role giving commands.

At the start of each cruise, when cadets are unfamiliar with the evolutions, it is particularly important that the chain of command be used so that each supervisor's span of control is small enough to monitor the assigned cadets effectively. Later, the upperclass cadets in the intermediate supervisory levels act as safety observers who give orders only by exception, such as stepping in if a line is improperly manned or if a problem develops. Leadership by exception is leadership in fact. It is typical of the organization of a warship in a high-threat environment where the extra seconds used in passing commands down the chain may be fatal.

A well-ordered chain of command is absolutely essential for successful sailing evolutions. Specific suggestions on organization are given for each evolution as it is discussed. The normal cadet chain of command used is:

1. Cadet Officer of the Deck (OOD)
2. Cadet Mast Captain
3. Pinrail and Fife Rail Captains
4. Line Captain
5. Other cadets

The Officer of the Deck oversees all evolutions and reports directly to the Commanding Officer. The Mast Safety Officers are responsible for their masts, ensuring that evolutions are safe and efficient and that proper training is being carried out.

The Mast Petty Officer is also a safety observer and works closely with the Cadet Mast Captain as a technical advisor.

SAFETY

Going to sea has always been inherently dangerous. Sailing a square-rigger can be particularly dangerous unless an attitude of safety consciousness is developed by each crew member. It is this attitude, more than any specific rules or regulations, that will ensure the safety of the vessel and her crew. For example, crew members must automatically make sure that watertight doors are properly dogged; if not, the door may swing out of control when the ship rolls or tacks. Also, port lights and weather deck doors must be properly dogged to prevent down flooding. Particular attention must be paid to housekeeping: gear left adrift can easily cause a bad fall if stepped on during a roll; or a book or sextant not secured can easily become a missile hazard. What might be harmless horseplay ashore becomes potentially dangerous skylarking at sea. In short, safety at sea is a way of life.

Safety Rules for Working Aloft and On Deck

1. Take no unnecessary chances and avoid grandstanding.

2. Always wear a safety belt. Until aloft, the clip should be hooked into the belt so that it cannot foul. Running rigging should never be used for support or for safety belts because it may become slack or may move. Standing rigging, *jackstays*, *safety stays*, and fixed pieces of gear

should be used instead. Most standing rigging is painted black.

3. One hand for the ship and one hand for yourself is the rule, even when wearing a safety belt. Both feet should be on the footropes or *flemish horses* at all times.

4. Always maintain at least three points of contact with standing rigging.

5. Hold onto the shrouds rather than the *ratlines*. Ratlines occasionally carry away, even with the best preventive maintenance.

6. Lay aloft only on the weather side. If a ratline carries away or you should lose your grip, the wind will blow you into the shrouds instead of overboard. This is particularly important as the ship heels.

7. Do not sit or stand on the yards. A sail in its gear or set may fly up and knock you off the yard.

8. In heavy winds, stay well clear of all headsail and staysail sheets. Parted sheets are extremely dangerous and can easily kill someone. Respect them!

9. Do not carry unnecessary gear aloft. Nametags, watches, hats, and the like must be left below. Gear that is carried aloft must be secured with a lanyard.

10. Do not lay out onto a yard unless it is securely in its fixed lifts and the braces are taut.

11. When going aloft on the mizzen, make sure that all radio transmitters in the combat information center (CIC), the radio room, and on the bridge are secured. Signs should be posted when transmitting.

12. While unfurling, the upper topsail should

not be thrown into its gear until cadets have laid in from the lower topsail, in case the sail blows in the face of those working on the lower topsail yard.

13. On deck, cadets assigned to headsail and staysail sheets must be particularly careful to control the sheets when setting and dousing. The blocks on the sheet, if not controlled, may easily gyrate and hit someone, hence the name "widow maker." The mizzen staysail sheets are particularly dangerous because of their close proximity to bridge personnel.

14. When handling lines, a sufficient number of cadets must be assigned according to wind conditions. Bad rope burns can easily occur if a line is undermanned, not to mention the potential damage to the gear.

15. Keep hands away from blocks when hauling lines and stand clear of bights. Lines can run so fast that a foot or an arm can be caught without warning in the block or a bight (loop in a line). Never straddle a line.

16. In all shipboard evolutions, and especially during sailing evolutions, absolute silence must be maintained except for necessary commands and reports.

17. While on the bowsprit, never work on the leeward side of a headsail because a sudden gust can easily knock a person overboard.

Overshadowing these individual safety rules are forehandedness and common sense: traits possessed by all good seamen and absolutely necessary for an officer standing watch. All hands must anticipate potential safety problems and take action to avoid them! Only through a forehanded appreciation of the inherent dangers of sailing and a strong spirit of safety consciousness can serious accidents be avoided. Safety is never to be sacrificed in favor of saving time or for convenience.

SETTING SAIL

Although almost all of the 190 lines on board are used when setting and dousing sail, the process is actually quite simple. Once the sails are *in their gear,* a good crew can set all sail in less than ten minutes and take in all sail in less than five. In contrast, an inexperienced crew may take well over an hour to set or douse.

The traditional order for setting square sails is from the bottom up, although the courses normally are set after the upper topsails. Thus, the order usually followed is:

1. Lower topsails
2. Upper topsails
3. Courses
4. Topgallants
5. Royals

Headsails and staysails are similarly set from the lowest to the highest. The mizzen staysail, however, is frequently not set because of its close proximity to the stack gas.

Sails are doused in reverse order. This order of setting and dousing reflects the natural order of taking in sails as winds increase. Normally, royals, topgallants, and upper staysails are taken in first, since they heel the ship excessively in high winds without adding significantly to *Eagle*'s speed. Courses are taken in before topsails because of their large size and the relative difficulty

Fig. 18. Upper topsail

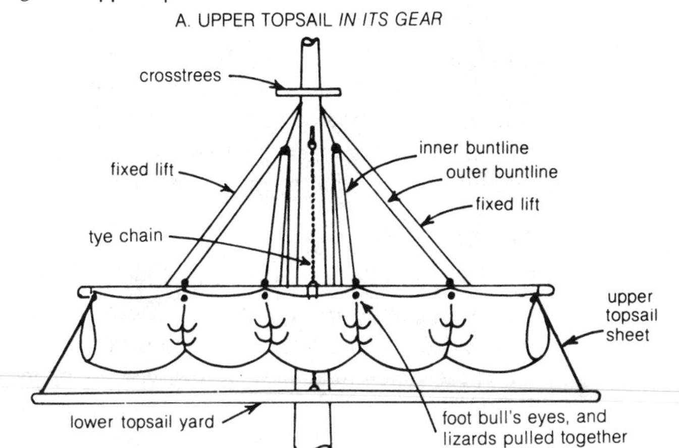

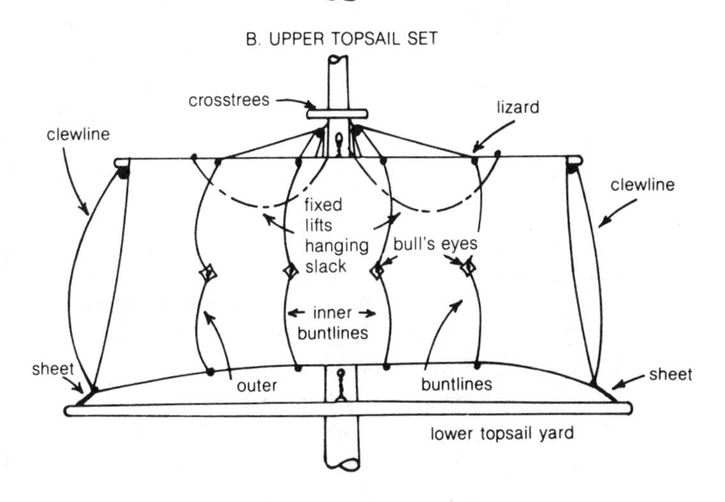

in handling them. In light winds, all staysails or headsails may be set or doused at the same time. The officer of the deck decides whether square sails or fore-and-aft sails are set first. The OOD, however, should make sure that sails are balanced on the three masts so that excessive rudder will not be needed to maintain course.

Unfurling

Before sails can be set, they must be unfurled. When furled, sails are secured by dacron straps called *gaskets,* which are used to secure the sail to the yard. When the cadet OOD gives the order to set sail, the mast captain will give the command, "*Lay aloft and loose all* (or a given) *sail.*" Before cadets actually lay aloft, the mast captain must ensure that the braces are taut and that the upper yards are in their fixed lifts. The mast captain should also ensure that all clewlines, buntlines, and leechlines are taut. If not, the sail may belly out when the gaskets are loosened, which may knock a person from the yard or tear gear. With an inexperienced crew or when in a moderate breeze, a yard captain should be assigned to supervise the unfurling aloft. On the command "*Let fall,*" the sail is pushed off the forward side of the yard and it is then *in its gear.* This command may be given by the mast captain, or it may be delegated to the yard captain. After the sail is in its gear, cadets lay in to the mast. Several cadets should remain aloft to *overhaul* the gear after all sails are set.

In light winds, two cadets on each yard are sufficient to unfurl sail. They should start at the yardarm and throw off gaskets as they work their way inboard to the mast. This procedure cannot be used in strong winds since the sail may belly out before all of the gaskets are clear and may jam the remaining gaskets. Moreover, with a single cadet on each yard, the sail will not be put into its gear all at once; it will slat about and possibly tear. Therefore, when in strong winds, or when time is critical, four to six cadets should be sent to each yard so that the entire sail can be thrown into its gear at the same time. The lower yards obviously require more cadets since the sails are much larger.

Setting Square Sails

The first step in setting all square sails is to "*sheet home,*" or haul the sail down to the next lowest yard, like a window shade, by hauling on the sheets and easing the clewlines. Since the sheets are opposed by the clewlines, buntlines, bunt-leechlines, and leechlines, these lines must be eased. They should be tended and not just thrown off, to ensure that they run freely and do not jam. In sheeting home, the clew of the sail should not be hauled down into the cheek block of the lower yard since it may jam. Several links of the sheet chain should remain visible when the sail is properly set. An equal amount of sheet chain should be showing on each side to allow the adjustable lifts to trim all five yards together.

The courses are a different matter, since they are the largest sails. On the command "sheet home," the course tacks and sheets are hauled, as appropriate, and the clewlines, buntlines, and leechlines are eased. In light winds, three or four cadets will be sufficient to man the tack and the sheet that take a strain. In strong winds, ten or more cadets may be needed to do the same job and a *stopper* will have to be passed on the sheet so that it can be safely belayed.

Common sense is called for in manning course tacks and sheets. When braced sharp, all of the strain will be on the weather tack and the lee sheet, and individual cadets can handle the remaining tack and sheet. When braced square, both sheets will have to be manned equally, with a single cadet tending each tack. When braced anywhere in between, cadets should be stationed as necessary according to the conditions.

Whenever the yards are braced sharp, the command "board the tack" should be given. The tack-jigger is used to haul the weather leech taut to ensure proper air flow across the leading edge of the sail. When the tack is boarded, the weather clew will lie forward of the yardarm and the leeward clew will lie aft of the leeward yardarm. With the wind abaft the beam, the tack is normally not boarded.

The sequence of commands in setting the *lower topsail* is:

1. Manning

a. Mast captain: "*Man the lower topsail gear.*"

b. Pinrail/fife rail captains (upperclass supervisors) will have underclass cadets man the clewlines and buntlines. Normally, the first cadet to reach a line is in charge of that line and is the "line captain." When the line is rigged for running and is properly manned, the line captain will report to the supervisor, "*Line manned and ready.*"

The upperclass supervisors will submit a consolidated report to the mast captain: "*Port pinrail manned and ready.*"

2. Setting

a. Mast captain to supervisors: "*On the lower topsail. Sheet home. Belay.*"

b. Pinrail captains: "*Ease the buntlines and clewlines.*"

c. Fife rail captain: "*Haul around on the sheets.*"

The other square sails are set similarly to this point. The courses are slightly different. The mast captain gives the command, "*Sheet home,*" and pinrail captains designate which lines shall be worked such as: "*Haul around on the weather tack and tend the lee sheet.*"

To complete setting the upper three sails, it is necessary to walk away with the halyard while continuing to ease the clewlines, buntlines, and bunt-leechlines. It is very important, however, that the lee brace (both braces for the upper topsail) be eased and the sheets of the sail above be thrown off to prevent binding. As you can see in figure 19, the upper topsail braces form the hypotenuse of a right triangle whose sides are the deck and the mast. As the yard is raised, the hypotenuse grows longer. Unless the braces are eased, the yard may bend or a brace may part. For this reason both braces for the upper topsail yards and the lee brace of the topgallants and royals must be eased as the yard is raised. The lead of the upper topsail braces keeps the yard

Fig. 19. Upper topsail braces

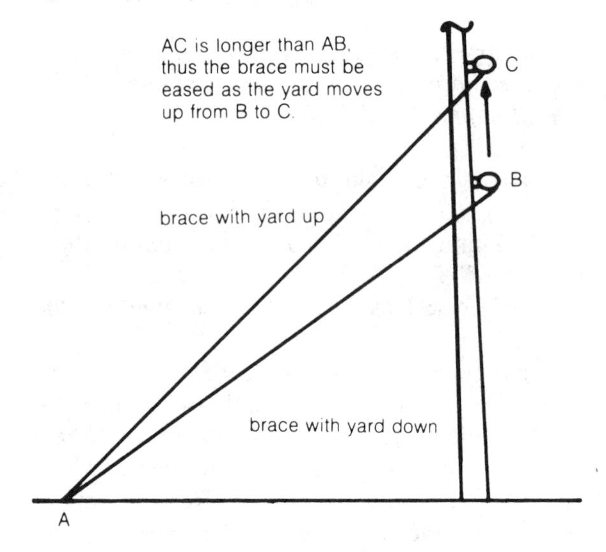

from being raised. Since the topgallant and royal braces are led from the mast astern, only the lee brace needs to be eased.

As you can see in figure 20, the sheets for a given sail are led along the yard below. As that yard is raised, the distance between C and D will increase and the sheet will pay out through the cloverleaf block at the center of the yard (C); the necessary slack will be taken up from the sheet at the yardarm (A-B). It might seem that what is lost at (A-B) is offset by what is gained at (C-D), so that no adjustment of the sheet would have to be made on deck, but this is not the case. Both (A-B) and (C-D) form the hypotenuses of right triangles. The lead of (A-B) is not quite vertical at the start; its angle increases if the yards are

Fig. 20. Sheets for a movable yard

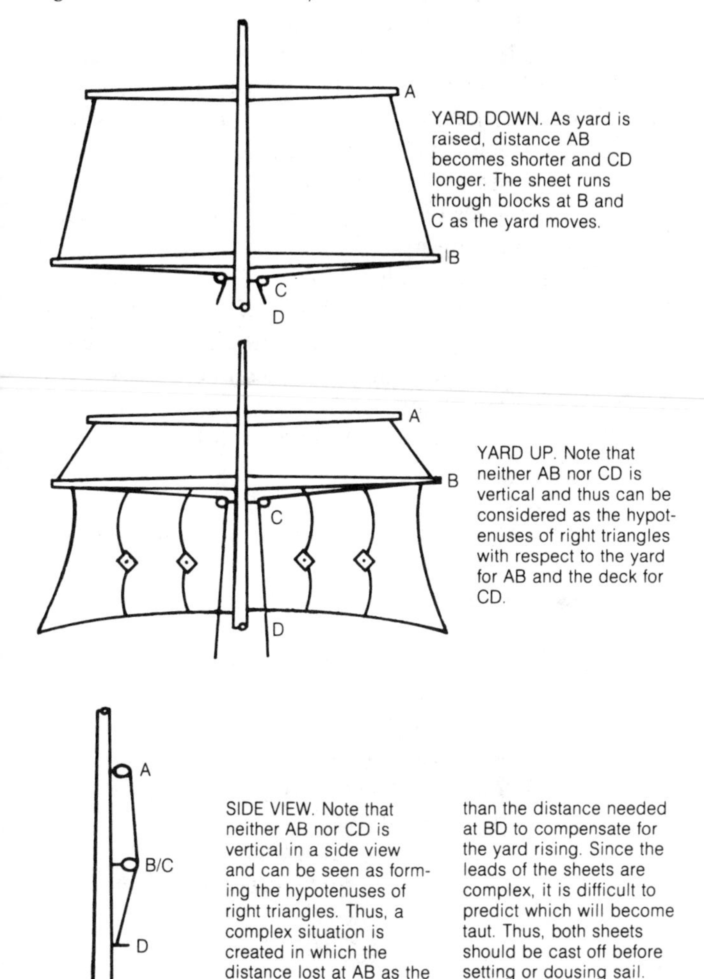

SIDE VIEW. Note that neither AB nor CD is vertical in a side view and can be seen as forming the hypotenuses of right triangles. Thus, a complex situation is created in which the distance lost at AB as the yard rises may be less than the distance needed at BD to compensate for the yard rising. Since the leads of the sheets are complex, it is difficult to predict which will become taut. Thus, both sheets should be cast off before setting or dousing sail.

fanned. Similarly, the inboard block (C) is actually a foot or more forward of the mast. Thus, the sheet leads down at an angle that depends on how far the yards are braced around. As a result, the distance lost at (A-B) often may be less than that needed at (C-D) as the yard goes up its track. Thus, the sheets will bind.

The leads of the sheets are geometrically complex, making it hard to predict which sheet will become taut at a given point of sail. Therefore, it is best to throw them both off when raising and lowering a yard to prevent the sheets from binding and possibly parting. Since the upper sail will not be set at this time, there is no strain on the sheets and there is no danger in throwing them off.

Once the sheets to the sail above have been thrown off, setting the upper square sails is simple. The halyard is hauled until the leeches are taut.

The sequence of commands for the upper three square sails is:

1. Manning and sheeting home are the same as with the lower topsail. After all stations are manned and ready and sheets for the sail above have been thrown off:

a. Mast captain to supervisors: "*On the main topgallant (royal, etc.). Sheet home. Belay.*"

b. Pinrail captains: "*Ease the buntlines, bunt-leechlines, and clewlines.*"

c. Fife rail captain: "*Haul around on the main topgallant sheets.*"

2. Raising the yard:

a. Mast captain: "*On the main topgallant. Walk away with the halyard.*" The appropriate pinrail captain should relay the command and then stand near the halyard to act as a safety observer. Buntlines and bunt-leechlines are tended. Clewlines are eased.

b. Mast captain to brace captain: "*Ease the lee topgallant brace*" or "*Ease the upper topsail braces.*" The brace captain should order the cadets on the braces to ease the braces enough so that the yard can go up easily but not enough to allow the yard to swing out of control. The brace captain should also adjust the braces to provide an appropriate fan. The weather brace is not eased on the royals and topgallants and should not be eased much on the upper topsail. If it is eased too much it may take up to a dozen cadets to haul against the force of the wind and correct the mistake of a single cadet. Not easing the brace enough, however, can cause binding, or even worse, a yard may be bent. Obviously, the brace captain plays an important role in setting or dousing sail.

c. Mast captain (when sail is almost set): "*Hand over hand the halyard. Belay.*" A stopper is always passed to belay the square sail halyards.

After all square sails are set it may be necessary to *overhaul* the gear. The weight of the buntlines and leechlines, especially in light air, may curl the foot of the sail. When overhauling, cadets should pull excess line aloft through the lizards so that there is slack in the buntlines, bunt-leechlines, and leechlines, allowing the sail to draw properly. These lines are then jammed under the jackstays to keep the strain off the foot of the sail, while still ensuring that the lines can be pulled free if hauled from on deck.

Setting Staysails and Headsails

Staysails and headsails are easier to set than the square sails. They are potentially much more dangerous, however, because of the whipping sheet blocks aptly called "widow makers." Staysail sheets are normally not rigged when the sails are furled. Thus, the first step in setting staysails is to rig the sheets on the appropriate tack and to put the sail into its gear. Particular care must be taken in rigging sheets since an error can easily result in a torn sail, even in moderate winds. Sheets must be led outboard of the stays and clear of the gantlines and other lines leading down the after side of the mast. The sheet for a staysail is always rigged aft and outboard of the staysail below it. Headsail sheets are permanently rigged and should always be ready for setting.

For setting, the downhauls and sheets are faked out for running and the halyard hauled until the luff of the sail is taut and no *scallops* are seen. Normally, at least four or five cadets are needed on a halyard, although in high winds, twice that number will be needed. If enough cadets are available, all headsails or staysails on a mast can be set simultaneously. As the sail is hauled up, the sheet should be tended, then sheeted home. If the sheet is too tight, it will bind the hanks against the stay and make it difficult to set the sail; if the sheets are slacked, the sheet block will slat about and may tear the sail or injure someone.

Thus, careful attention is needed during the entire process. In light winds, one or two cadets are needed on a sheet. In high winds, three or four will be needed to tend the sheet and several more to sheet it home when the halyard is hauled taut. Since headsails and staysails are particularly difficult to handle in high winds, insufficient manning may easily result in bad rope burns. In high winds, it may be necessary to use a rattail jigger to sweat the sheet home.

Sail trim is discussed in chapter 5. The sails must be trimmed in enough, however, so the sheet of an upper sail does not chafe against a lower sail, as such chafing will quickly wear through the sail. Staysails are frequently trimmed in too far. Sheeting the staysails flat will not necessarily result in more driving power, and a fore-and-aft sail that is trimmed in too far will actually stall the vessel and result in more leeway than driving power.

When trimming, the sheets are eased until the sail luffs, and then they are sheeted in to the point where the sail draws again. Also, the wire rope pendant of the weather sheet on the headsails (which does not have any strain) will quickly chafe through if it is allowed to lay on the forestays. Thus, after the headsails are set, the weather headsail sheet pendants and their blocks should be passed over the stays. As a result, the manila sheet, which can more easily stand the chafing, will lie on the stay.

As already mentioned, fore-and-aft sail sheets

tend to gyrate if they are not carefully controlled when the sail is being set or doused. As a result, everyone should stand well clear of the staysail (and headsail) sheet blocks when handling those sails.

The sequence of commands in setting headsails and staysails is:

1. Mast captain (after all have reported manned and ready): "*On the flying jib. Ease the downhaul. Tend the sheet. Haul around on the halyard.*" In complex evolutions like tacking, the mast captain may delegate the setting of the staysails to an upperclass supervisor, in which case the mast captain will give just the command "*Set the staysails or headsails,*" and the supervisor will give the rest of the commands.

2. Mast captain (when the sail is almost set): "*Hand over hand the halyard. Belay. Sheet home.*" The pinrail captain will then properly trim the sail by the sheet without further command.

Setting the Spanker

Setting the spanker is quite easy. The boom must first be topped about two feet so that the sail can be set without damaging its leech, and the *preventer* must be rigged on the leeward side. The boom is then positioned for setting by hauling on the preventer while easing the sheet, weather vang, and weather flag halyard. Normally, unless the ship is rolling heavily, three or four cadets will suffice on the preventer and one each on the remaining lines. Once the boom is positioned, the sail is set by hauling on the outhauls while easing the inhauls and brails.

Since the spanker is one of the largest sails, many cadets are needed to set it. A single cadet can handle all of the brails on one side; similarly, one cadet is sufficient for each inhaul. At least three cadets are needed on the peak outhaul and five cadets on the foot outhaul, although more are preferable.

The sequence of commands in setting the spanker is:

1. Preliminary steps after sail is loosened. (All medium frequency and high frequency transmitters must be secured before sending cadets aloft on the mizzen.)

 a. Mast captain: "*Man the spanker gear. Rig the preventer.*"

 b. Mast captain (when all is ready): "*Ease the sheet. Haul around on the topping lift. Belay.*"

 c. Mast captain: "*Ease the sheet. Tend the vangs and flag halyard. Haul around on the preventer.*"

2. Setting the spanker:

 a. Mast captain: "*Ease the peak and foot inhauls and the brails. Haul around on the peak and foot outhauls.*"

 b. Mast captain (when all scallops have been removed from the head and foot): "*That's well. Belay the spanker gear.*"

Setting the Gaff Topsail

The gaff topsail is set much like a staysail. The halyard hauls the sail up while the sheet hauls the clew out to the end of the gaff. The clewline, like a downhaul, is eased. The tack is tended and then used to trim the luff and foot of the sail after the halyard and sheet have been belayed. Three or four cadets are sufficient for the halyard and sheet; a single cadet can handle the clewline and another the tack.

The sequence of commands in setting the gaff topsail is:

Mast captain: "*On the gaff topsail. Ease the clewline. Tend the tack. Haul around on the halyard. Sheet home.*"

It should be noted that in giving commands for setting sails, the commands to "ease" and "tend" are always given before the command to "haul" on any line. This is because almost every line is opposed by another and before you can haul on one line another must be eased or gear may tear or part.

DOUSING SAIL

Taking in Square Sails

The procedure for taking in a square sail is the reverse of that for setting it: those lines that were eased in setting are hauled, and those lines that were hauled are now eased. The first step for the upper three sails is to ease the halyard to bring the yard down into its lifts and spill most of the wind from the sail.

It might appear that the great weight of the yards and their sails would bring them down easily when the halyard is eased, but this is sometimes not the case. The entire force of the wind on the sail is concentrated on the yard shoe, which rides on a track on the forward side of the mast. This tremendous pressure, even in moderate winds, often binds the shoe against the track and prevents the yard from being lowered. Thus, it is necessary to haul the yard down using the only available lines, the clewlines. On the command "*Clew down,*" the sheets remain belayed, the halyard is eased, and clewlines hauled. The sheets for the sail above are thrown off to prevent any possible binding, and the braces, which were eased in setting, are rounded in.

When the yard is securely in its lifts, the sail is hauled up into its gear. On the command "*Clew up,*" sheets are eased, and clewlines, buntlines, and bunt-leechlines are hauled until the sail is up to the yard. On the courses, the process is the same, except that tacks must also be eased and the command is "*Rise tacks and sheets.*" The lower topsail, which is bent to a fixed yard, is taken in by merely clewing up.

Two cadets should man each halyard. A single cadet can usually man the sheets, and each brace. In light winds, three cadets will be needed for each clewline and at least one for each buntline and bunt-leechline. On the courses and on other sails, more cadets must be added to each line as the wind increases, with the majority being added to the clewlines.

The sequence of commands for taking in a square sail is:

1. Preparatory steps:

a. Fake the halyard and sheets free for running, since a jam could result in the sail slatting about violently and possibly tearing.

b. Throw off the sheets for the sail above (upper topsail and topgallant only).

c. Clear away the tack-jigger on the courses.

2. Lowering the yards (upper three sails):

a. Mast captain: "*Clew down.*"

b. Pinrail captain: "*Ease the halyard. Haul around on the clewlines.*" Buntlines and buntleechlines are tended as the yard comes down. The cadets on the halyard must keep at least a half turn on the pin to keep the halyard from running out of control and the yard from crashing down into its lifts.

c. Brace captain: "*Round in the lee brace*" (both braces on the upper topsail). For the topgallants and royals, rounding in just the lee brace and leaving the weather brace belayed will make resetting sail simple. If the yards were properly fanned before they were lowered, they will be fanned again when the sails are reset if only the lee brace has been handled.

3. Taking in the sail:

a. Mast captain: "*On the fore royal (topgallant, etc.). Clew up.*" This command should be given as soon as the lifts come taut and the cadet on the halyard sounds off "*Slack on deck.*" Ideally the cadets on the clewlines will continue hauling as the sheets are eased, although with an inexperienced crew this may not be possible.

Since the lower topsails have no halyard, "*Clew up*" is the only command necessary. For the courses, "*Rise tacks and sheets*" is the proper command, and the clew-garnets are hauled instead of clewlines.

b. Fife rail captain: "*On the fore royal. Ease the sheets.*" Cadets must ease the sheets in a lively fashion since one cadet holding a sheet can easily check a half dozen hauling on the clewlines.

c. Pinrail captain: "*On the fore royal. Haul around on the clewlines, buntlines, and buntleechlines.*" The pinrail captains must carefully monitor the dousing of the sail and be prepared to order, "*That's well*" on each line as the sail is hauled up to the yard. The lines usually come up at different rates and hauling on a line when the sail is already in its gear may tear out a bull's eye or jam a clew block. The mast captain is generally a safety observer and also ensures that no lines are being hauled after they are two-blocked and makes sure that no lines jam.

Dousing Headsails and Staysails

The headsails and staysails are doused by easing the halyard, tending the sheet, and hauling around on the downhaul. The sheets must be handled carefully. If slacked, the sail will slat about and perhaps tear, and the sheet blocks will whip around dangerously. On the other hand, if the sheets are too taut, it will be difficult to haul the sail down, since the hanks will bind to the stay. The downhaul runs from the fife rail to the head of the sail and then to the clew.

In dousing, therefore, the sheet should be held until the head of the sail is hauled down to the miter seam. Holding the sheet allows the sheet to oppose the downhaul so that the head of the sail can be hauled down to the miter seam and collapse the top half of the sail. Then the sheet should be eased to allow the sail to be completely doused. Obviously, careful coordination between the pinrail captains and the downhaul supervisor is needed throughout the operation.

Usually, a single cadet is needed for each halyard and sheet. As few as two or three cadets can handle the downhauls, although more are preferable to get the sail down quickly. Cadets should be assigned to walk down the sheets for the mizzen staysails to protect those working on the bridge. If enough personnel are available, all staysails on a mast may be doused at once. Whenever handling the main topmast staysail, the main mast captain should station cadets on the boat deck to ensure that it doesn't tear on the accommodation ladder or brows.

The commands for dousing fore-and-aft sails are simple:

Mast captain: "*Ease the halyard. Tend the sheet. Haul around on the downhaul.*"

Brailing in the Spanker

Brailing in the spanker is much like clewing up on a square sail: outhauls are eased, inhauls and brails hauled. After the sail is brailed in, the boom is cradled and the preventer struck. At least three cadets are needed on the peak inhaul, five on the foot inhaul, and one for each brail. Because of the size of the spanker, more cadets are preferred.

The sequence of commands for brailing in the spanker is:

1. Brailing in:

a. Mast captain: "*Ease the outhauls. Haul around on the inhauls and brails.*"

2. Securing:

a. Mast captain: "*Ease the preventer. Tend the vangs and flag halyard. Haul around on the sheet.*"

b. Mast captain: "*Ease the topping lift. Haul around on the sheets.*" And if no sailing is to be done in the near future, "*Strike the preventer.*"

Special care should be taken when handling the topping lift because of the tremendous weight of the spanker boom. Also, the boom is not lowered until it is amidships and the chock, which is a heavy wooden cradle, is in place.

Dousing the Gaff Topsail

The gaff topsail is doused much like a staysail. The halyard and sheet are eased and the clewline hauled. The tack usually has little strain on it and can be left untended. Two or three cadets are needed for the clewline, and one each to tend the halyard and sheet.

The commands are simple:

Mast captain: "*On the gaff topsail. Ease the halyard and sheet. Haul around on the clewline.*"

FURLING SAIL

In light air, it is permissible to leave the sails in their gear without furling. In stronger winds, the sails would slat about and quickly chafe; thus they must be furled. There are two types of furl: the sea furl, used when appearance is not a factor, and the harbor furl, when it is.

Sea Furling Square Sails

Furling is an art more easily learned from practice than described in a text. Figures 21–26 illustrate the proper way to furl a square sail. In heavy winds, when there is danger of the sail slatting about, cadets should be stationed in the crosstrees and tops so they may immediately lay out onto the yards when the sails are up in their gear. Under such conditions, the weather side of the sail must be smothered first so gusts cannot catch the weather leech and cause the sail to belly out of the hands of the cadets who are trying to furl it.

To achieve a tight furl, the sail must be completely clewed up to the yard. Care must be taken not to jam a clew in the clew block nor to pull the lizards for the buntlines and bunt-leechlines above the yard, where they will impede furling. The leech of the sail should be brought up parallel to the yard and held there until the last bight is dropped (as shown in figure 21) in case an awkward tangle of sail is created at the leeches.

In furling an arm's-length bight of sail is taken simultaneously by all cadets on the yard. It is pulled up and held against the yard. As subsequent bights are taken, the earlier ones are dropped into it, until the entire sail has been taken up and the last few feet of the sail (at the head) form a tight skin. The entire sail is then rolled up onto the yard and set between the jackstay and the safety stay. Gaskets should then be passed over the sail and secured to the safety stay.

It is important that cadets not use any hitches that will jam in securing the gaskets, for it will be impossible to loosen the gaskets without cutting them. Generally, a slip clove hitch is used. Care must be taken to ensure that there are no *deadmen* and that gaskets are snug to prevent the sail from working loose.

Fig. 21. Furling a square sail

A. Clew up (after clewing down) leechlines, buntlines, and clewlines coming up. Note leech ahead.

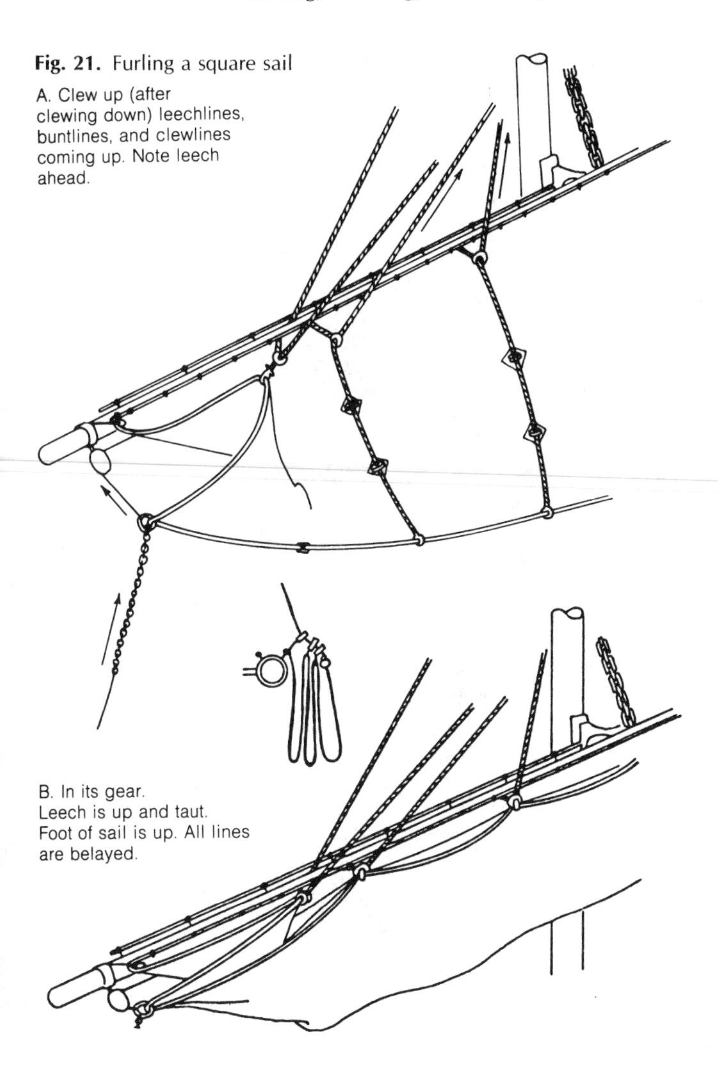

B. In its gear. Leech is up and taut. Foot of sail is up. All lines are belayed.

Fig. 22. Yard manned. Note cadet keeping leech up on yard. Foot pulled up to yard.

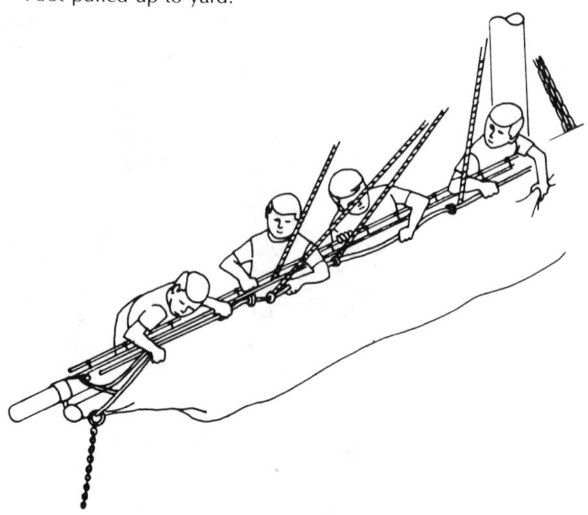

Fig. 23. Furling. Cadets must keep together, lifting each bight uniformly. Outboard continues to keep leech up on yard.

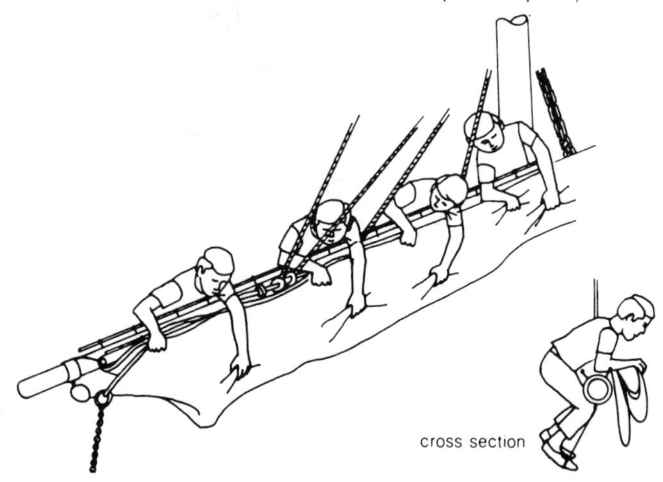

Harbor Furling Square Sails

When appearance is important, as when entering port, sails are usually harbor furled. The process is basically the same as sea furling but is more time consuming. The clew of the sail is brought up tight and the leech held against the yard. The foot of the sail, however, is held against the yard and the buntlines eased out so that the sail hangs in a single large bight. Forearm-length bights are then taken and held, layer by layer, against the yard. The final bight is drawn tightly over the rest of the sail to form a smooth skin and the sail is pulled up on top of the yard. After the sail has been furled, buntlines and leechlines may be stopped off to the mast to give a neater appearance.

Fig. 24. Sail almost furled. Drop each bight into the following bight until a tight skin is attained. Drop leech and foot just before the last bight is taken. Roll sail up on yard.

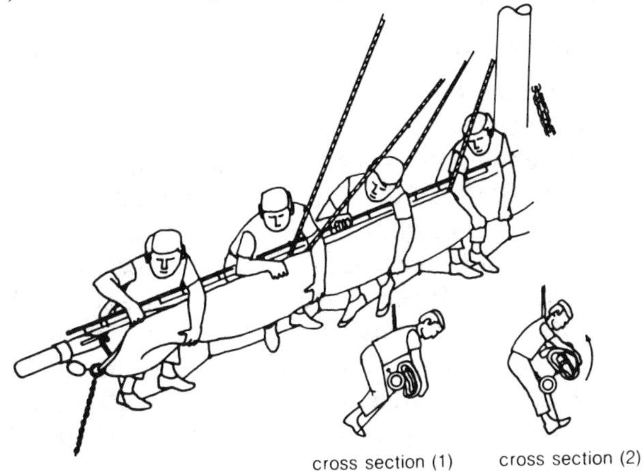

Proper harbor furling requires near-calm conditions and close coordination. It is best to assign a yard captain to coordinate the taking of the bights. A good harbor furl will be perfectly smooth and will not be seen from on deck aft of the mast.

Sea Furling Fore-and-Aft Sails

All fore-and-aft sails are furled in basically the same way. Cadets should lay out on the crane lines on either side of the sail and furl the sail into itself until it is tight enough for gaskets to be passed and until the remaining sail material can form a protective skin around the rest of the sail. Gaskets are then passed around the sail.

Although two cadets can sea furl a fore-and-aft sail, the process is much easier if a cadet is stationed on each crane line so the whole sail can be furled simultaneously. Headsails are furled in much the same way but gaskets are passed over the bowsprit. Cadets should always lay out on the bowsprit on the weather side.

Harbor Furling Fore-and-Aft Sails

In harbor furling a staysail, the first step is to shake the sail out so that it hangs freely. Then, locate the miter seam which runs from the clew to the center of the luff. The seam must be positioned vertically along the after side of the sail. The body of the sail is then furled inward from either side. When furled, the miter seam is still vertical and directly aft, and the entire sail forms a smooth cylinder. The bottom of the furl should be neatly squared off. Gaskets should not be pulled so tightly as to disturb the tube shape of the furl.

Fig. 25. Furling the staysail

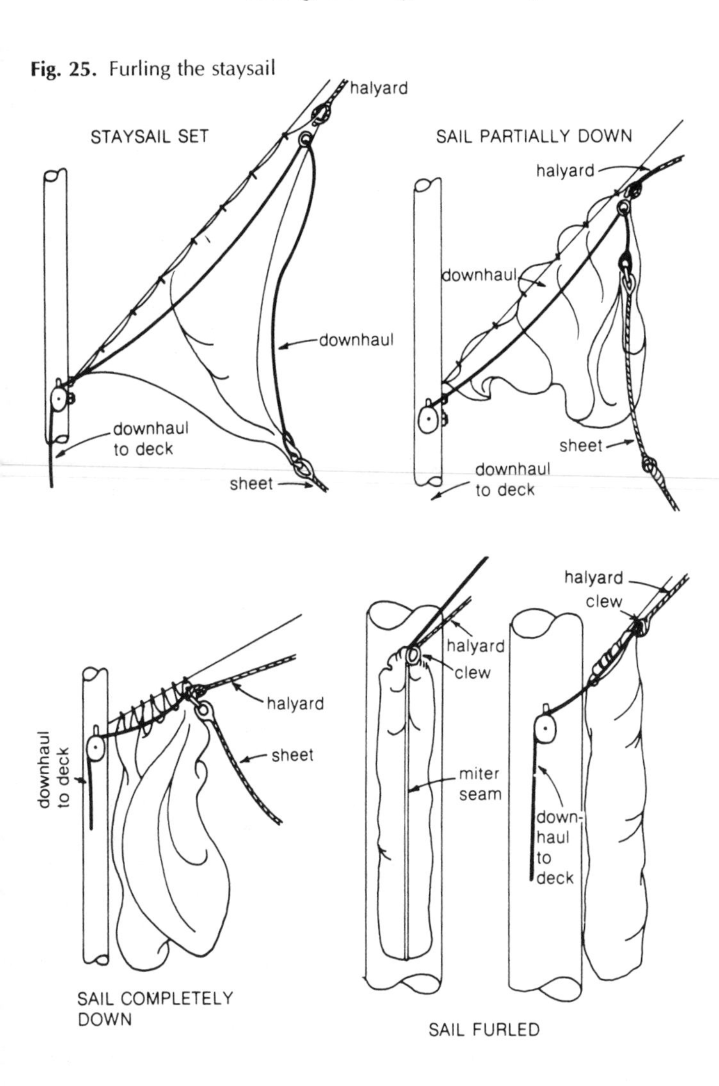

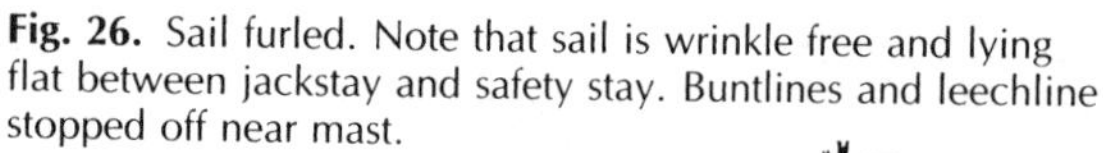
Fig. 26. Sail furled. Note that sail is wrinkle free and lying flat between jackstay and safety stay. Buntlines and leechline stopped off near mast.

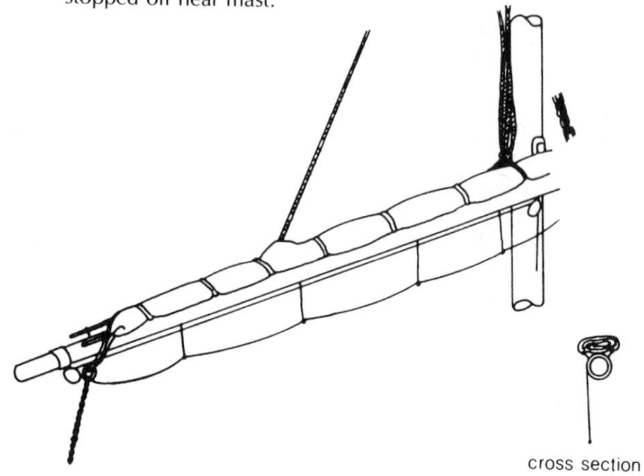

Figure 25 illustrates the sequence of dousing a staysail and its appearance when doused. Headsails are harbor furled similarly and gaskets are secured to the bowsprit.

Furling the Spanker and Gaff Topsail

The spanker is harbor furled exactly like a staysail except that there is no miter seam. A good furl resembles a tight cylinder. Since the foot of the sail is longer than the peak, there will be excess material at the foot. This material should be tucked in neatly so that only a tight skin can be seen.

The gaff topsail is an awkward sail to harbor furl. Like the spanker, it is bulkier along the gaff. The sail should be tucked in so that a tight outer skin remains and so that as little sail as possible can be seen from on deck.

TRIMMING SAIL ▪ 5

Trimming sail to maximize ship speed is one of the greatest challenges for the officer of the deck, requiring constant attention and a true sense of wind and sea and their combined effect on *Eagle*. The cadet OOD and cadet BMOW (boatswain's mate of the watch) work together closely to ensure that sails are properly trimmed and that every wind shift is taken advantage of.

Trimming sail requires a feel for the wind and sea as well as an understanding of some basic principles. Square sails are trimmed with the braces, sheets, and course lifts; fore-and-aft sails are trimmed with their sheets. Before discussing trimming and sail balance, it is necessary to understand some of the basic forces involved.

SAILING FORCES

The combination of forces acting on *Eagle* to propel her through the water is complex and difficult to analyze. For the purposes of trimming, however, only a few of these forces are discussed.

Aerodynamic Force

Sails derive the bulk of their power from aerodynamic lift. A sail presents an aspect to the wind much like that of an airplane wing. The wind must flow faster across the curved leeward side than across the aerodynamically flat windward side (fig. 27). In accordance with Bernoulli's principle, a low pressure area that pulls the sail forward is created. The direction of this force

Fig. 27. Aerodynamic lift

A. Aircraft wing. The air must pass more quickly over the top of the wing than the bottom and thus the pressure is lowered and lift created.

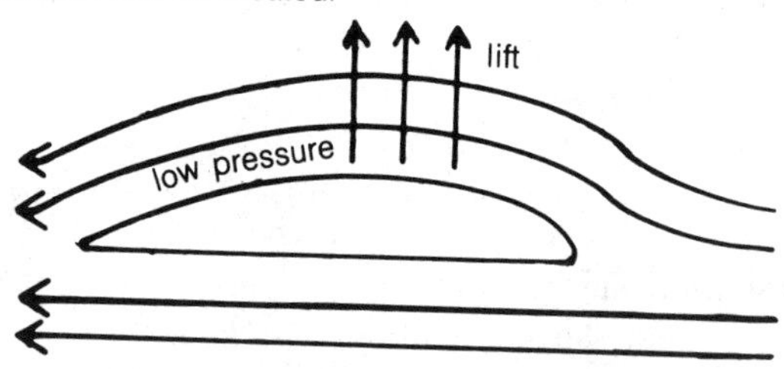

B. Sail. Airflow is the same as with a wing and a low pressure area and lift are created on the leeward side of the sail.

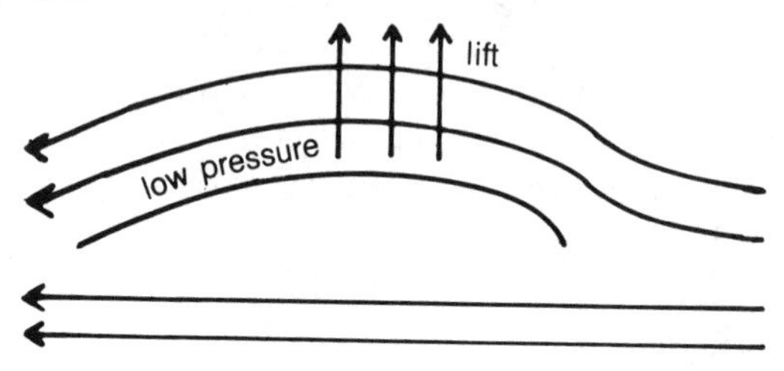

C. Slot effect. The inner jib forces more wind through the slot, lowering pressure and increasing lift. The total lift with a proper slot exceeds that of both sails acting without a slot.

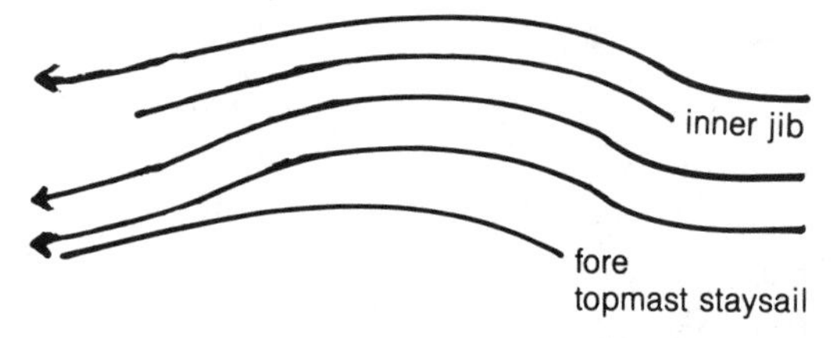

can be divided into an athwartships component that causes heel and leeway and a fore-and-aft component that draws the ship forward and therefore drives the ship. The athwartships component is countered by the lateral resistance of the keel of the ship, which reduces leeway to a minimum.

Sails are trimmed so that the leading edge forms an acute angle of attack with the wind so that there is a smooth airflow across both sides of the sail. Air flows from the luff to the leech on fore-and-aft sails and from the weather leech to the leeward leech on a square sail. When this angle is improper, turbulence or aerodynamic drag is created instead of lift, causing the sail to stall. If the wind is too far forward, the sail will lift or luff.

The Slot Effect

For fore-and-aft sails, there is a second important factor: the *slot effect*. The close proximity of the headsails and staysails to each other, when they are properly trimmed, forces the wind through the slot between the sails at a much faster rate than if the sails were separated. This greater speed lowers the pressure on the leeward side of the sail and increases lift and drive. Thus, staysails and especially headsails must be carefully trimmed to each other as well as to the wind.

Driving Force

For aerodynamic lift to be a factor, the wind must form an acute angle of attack with the leading edge of the sail. Therefore, when sailing off the wind such as a broad reach, aerodynamic effects are reduced until when running downwind there is no air flow across the sail and the sail does not act as an airfoil any longer. Thus, when the ship is running downwind, the wind actually drives the ship forward by creating a driving force on the sail area it encounters. Driving force can only be increased by adding sail area. Sails are kept perpendicular to the wind to maximize this driving force.

Center of Effort

Each sail has a center of effort, groups of sails such as headsails or all fore square sails have a center of effort, and there is a total center of effort for all sails set. The concept of center of effort is important to understand when dealing with sail balance.

Center of Lateral Resistance

The center of lateral resistance is the center of the resistance to leeway created by the underwater body of the ship. For smaller vessels, this is usually a centerboard or some type of keel. *Eagle* has a full-length keel. The center of lateral resistance changes with heel as the wetted surface area changes.

TRIMMING FORE-AND-AFT SAILS

Fore-and-aft sails derive the bulk of their power from aerodynamic lift. In general, fore-and-aft sails are trimmed like the sails on a sloop or other fore-and-aft rigged vessel would be. Most of the power is created in the first few feet of the luff, so it is particularly important that the halyard be hauled taut so that the luff has no *scallops* that would interfere with a smooth airflow. The sheet should be eased until the sail luffs and then sheeted back to the point where it stops luffing. All sails on a mast are trimmed to the wind and then to each other so that they do not backwind each other and ruin the slot effect.

The spanker and gaff topsail are trimmed like the other fore-and-aft sails. They are joined through their leeches and therefore trimmed together. The aerodynamic effects of the spanker are the same, but because of its distance from the pivot point, the spanker can produce a large turning moment and excessive weather helm if trimmed improperly. It is one of the largest sails, however, and can produce tremendous driving power when trimmed properly. If excessive weather helm is observed, the OOD should first ensure that all sails forward are properly trimmed before easing the spanker sheet or brailing it in.

The headsails and the main staysails must also be trimmed in relationship to the square sails. Since yards can only be braced 45 degrees to the ship, the square sails require *Eagle* to sail off the wind farther than would be required for a vessel with fore-and-aft sails alone. Therefore, the fore-and-aft sails must be trimmed accordingly. If they are sheeted too flat, they will cause more leeway than driving power.

When *on the wind,* the headsails and main staysails usually backwind the lower square sails. Although this may seem counterproductive, the driving power gained by the fore-and-aft sails usually offsets the loss of drive in the lower square sails. In short, the effect of each sail on all others must be considered. In setting, dousing, and trimming sails, the OOD must consider all of these effects to produce the best overall speed for the ship.

Fore-and-aft sails also produce driving force when the wind is from astern and aerodynamic force is no longer a factor. This force, however, is not nearly as significant since most of the sail area of the fore-and-aft sails is blanketed by the square sails when running downwind and since the fore-and-aft sails present relatively little sail area to the wind. The spanker is the exception since the spanker boom can be used to haul the spanker to port or starboard.

TRIMMING SQUARE SAILS

The driving power of square sails can be explained in terms of simple vector diagrams. The wind that strikes the sails is not the *true wind* but a relative wind, a combination of the true wind and a wind vector produced by the ship's motion through the water. As diagrammed in figure 28, the relative wind is always forward of the true wind. The faster the ship moves in relation to the true wind, the farther forward the relative wind. The sails are always trimmed to this relative wind rather than to the true wind. This is a fairly simple task since the ship's flags and pennants provide *telltales* that indicate the relative rather than the true wind. The relative wind can be different on each mast.

Aerodynamic considerations are present and significant when the relative wind is near or forward of the beam. When *Eagle* is close-hauled,

Fig. 28. Relative wind

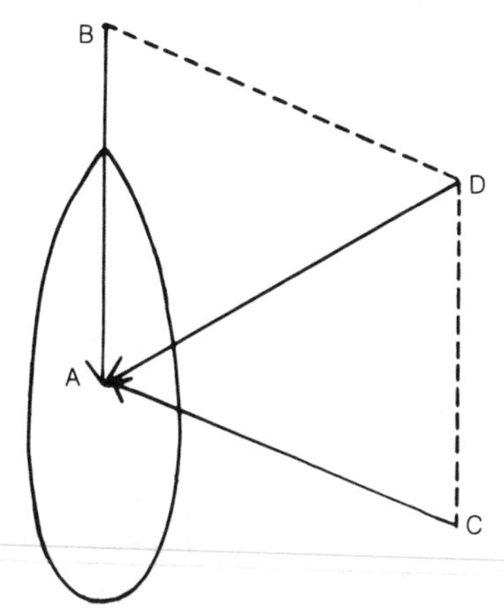

AB Motion of the ship creates a relative wind directly opposite to the direction of the ship's motion and equal to its speed.

AC True wind.

AD Resultant relative wind that strikes the sail. The stronger the relative wind AB, the farther forward will be the resultant relative wind AD.

the angle of attack of a square sail is very similar to that of a staysail. The leading edge of a square sail is the weather leech, analogous to the luff of a staysail. As with fore-and-aft sails, the leading edge (weather leech) should form an acute angle with the relative wind as does an airplane wing. Although a fore-and-aft sail will lift along its luff, a square sail lifts along the weather leech when the ship gets too close to the wind.

As seen in figure 29A, when the relative wind (AD) strikes a square sail, part of its energy (AE) can be considered as acting along the sail. This energy is not available for driving the ship. The

Fig. 29. Driving force

A. The effect of the relative wind and the resultant driving force on the square sails.

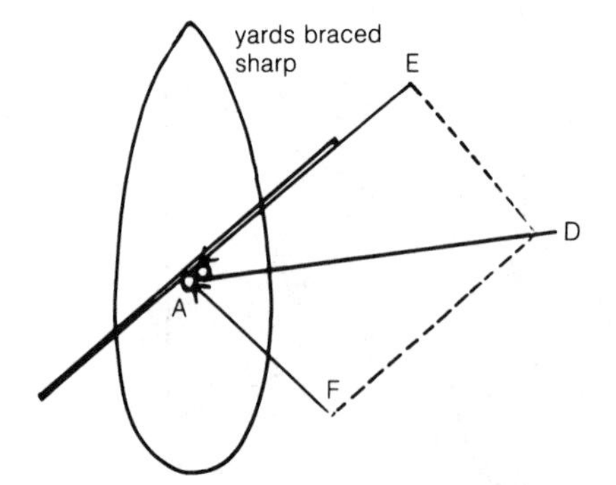

AE The component of the relative wind AD acting parallel to the sails

AF The driving force component of the relative wind AD acting against the sails (does not include aerodynamic force)

B. The relative driving force AF for different angles of the relative wind AD to the sails

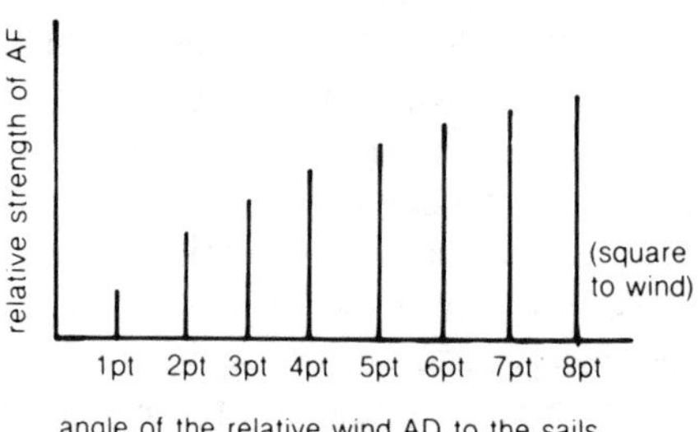

rest of the wind's energy (AF) acts at right angles to the sails and drives the ship forward. The combination of aerodynamic lift and this driving force (AF) results in energy provided by the square sails. The force (AF) is actually pushing the ship forward and therefore with the wind abaft the beam all possible sail that will carry should be set. As can be seen in figure 29B, AF is maximized with the sails square to the wind. Unfortunately, this gain is offset by the loss of aerodynamic forces and the loss of the fore-and-aft sail area when the wind is abaft the beam. This driving force is the only force available, however, and the square sails must provide the bulk of the driving power when running downwind.

A third consideration is the energy applied at right angles to the sails. In figure 30, part of the energy applied to the sails imparts a force at a

Fig. 30. The effect of relative force AF on ship movement

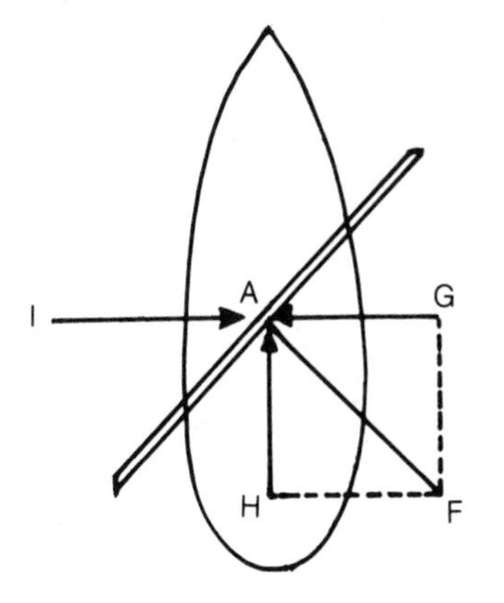

AF The effective force of the wind on the sails.
AG The component of the effective wind acting laterally causing leeway and heel.
AH The component of the effective wind driving the ship forward.
AI Center of lateral resistance—the effective force (created by the keel and underwater body) that resists leeway

right angle to the ship's head. This force (AG) is opposed by the great resistance of the full keel to lateral motion through the water (AI), or the center of lateral resistance. Therefore, the ship resists moving sideways through the water (leeway) and the resistance of the keel translates energy into forward motion (AH). *Eagle*'s keel acts like a centerboard does in a small boat, resisting leeway and thus forcing the ship to take the path of least resistance, which is forward.

PRACTICAL TRIMMING

As previously discussed, both square and fore-and-aft sails are trimmed to form an acute angle of attack with the wind whenever the wind is forward of the quarter. This ensures smooth airflow across the sails and maximizes aerodynamic force. The diagram in figure 31A represents the angle of trim for the yards based on changes in the relative wind. This table is just a starting point and cannot be exact since practical trimming depends on many factors, including wind velocity, heel of the ship, sea condition, and others. Yards are normally trimmed one point at a time, as shown in figure 31A. When *braced sharp*, the yards form an angle of about 45 degrees, or four points, to the ship's head. At 90 degrees to the ship the yards are *braced square*. The intermediate points are named by their distance forward of being braced square: square, one point on a starboard tack, two points on a starboard tack, three points on a starboard tack, braced sharp. It is possible to brace the upper yards farther than the lower yards. This is not done, however, because when braced sharp, yards are *fanned,* as is described later.

Fig. 31. Trimming the square sails

A. Positions of the yards when trimming square sails

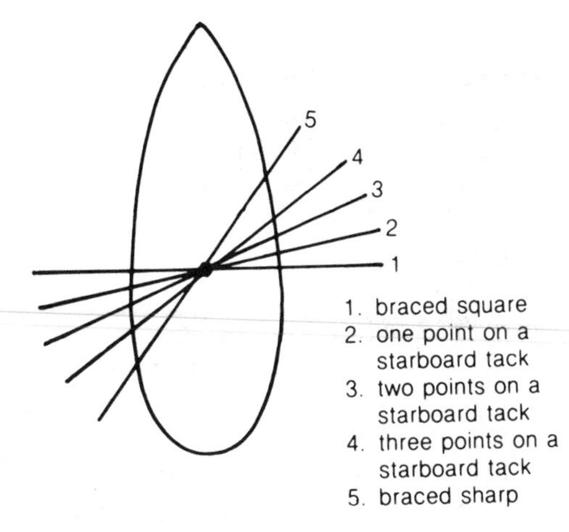

B. Theoretical optimum trim for square sails to maximize the combined driving force and aerodynamic force for different points of sail

Relative wind	*Best trim of yards*	*Angle of yards to relative wind*
045 (broad on bow)	sharp	½
056 ¼ (3pts fwd of beam)	sharp	1 point
067 ½ (2pts fwd of beam)	sharp	2 points
078 ¾ (1pt fwd of beam)	sharp	3 points
090 (abeam)	sharp	4 points
101 ¼ (1pt aft the beam)	sharp–3 points	4–5 points
112 ½ (2pts aft the beam)	3 points	5 points
123 ¾ (3pts aft the beam)	2–3 points	5–6 points
135 (broad on the quarter)	2 points	6 points
146 ¼ (3pts on quarter)	2 points	7 points
157 ½ (2pts on quarter)	1–2 points	7–8 points
168 ¾ (1pt on quarter)	1 point	8 points
180 (astern)	square	8 points

As you can see in figure 31, *Eagle* cannot sail closer than about 75 degrees to the true wind. This point of sail is called *close-hauled* and is where *Eagle* sails the fastest. This is the only point of sail where all twenty-two sails are drawing and where the combination of aerodynamic force and driving force is maximized.

As the wind draws abaft the beam, ship's speed decreases. The yards should be left sharp until the wind draws aft of the beam and then slowly braced back until they are square to the ship when the wind is dead astern. Until the wind is on the quarter, the yards form an acute angle with the wind. This develops maximum driving power, allowing a smooth airflow across the sails, and minimizes turbulence. This maximizes the combination of driving and aerodynamic forces. Yards are *fanned* with the wind near or forward of the beam to account for the increase in relative wind speed striking the higher sails.

After the wind draws aft of the quarter, aerodynamic effects are minimal and the wind actually has to drive the ship forward; therefore yards are braced square to the wind. This is the slowest point of sail because aerodynamic force is no longer present and the main square sails *blanket* those on the fore. Also, the fore-and-aft sails will no longer fill properly when running downwind and sometimes must be doused. The mainsail is often *goosewinged* or even doused in such circumstances to allow wind to pass through to the fore sails. In light air, the sheets on the main square sails are sometimes "soft-sheeted," to allow even more wind to pass through to the fore. Yards are stacked and cockbill removed (see below). Sometimes when running downwind, it is advantageous to brace the fore yards square and brace the main yards to two or three points to attempt to keep the square sails on both masts filled and driving.

If the sails are not set the yards should still be braced sharp. This is especially true when motoring into the wind, when there may be a difference of up to a knot in speed depending on whether the yards are braced to the wind or boxed against it.

Understanding Cockbill and Fanning

There are two other elements that must be considered in trimming square sails. As the ship heels in a wind, the yards will *cockbill* with respect to the horizon (the horizontal). As a result, the wind, which travels essentially parallel to the water's surface, will not strike the sails and flow smoothly off to leeward. Instead it will flow at an angle up and over the yards, causing an excessive amount of turbulence and a drop in efficiency and speed. Thus, the yards must be trimmed parallel to the horizon. All sails can be adjusted at once by using the course lifts that are connected to the remaining yards through the leeches of the sails. In adjusting a movable lift, the lee course sheet and tack must be eased as the yard moves up while the weather sheet and tack are rounded in. The leeward braces on the lower three yards will also have to be eased since they will bind as the lee lift is hauled.

Fanning is the trimming process by which the weather yardarms are progressively braced farther back for each higher yard. The purpose of fanning is to allow each sail to present the optimum angle of attack to the wind. The true wind speed increases slightly with height above the water because of the lessening effect of the surface friction of the water. As the true wind increases with respect to the ship's speed, the relative wind that strikes the royal will be farther aft of that that strikes the courses. Fanning allows each sail to be properly set to the relative wind at its height.

Sometimes, the topgallants and royals are fanned back even more than is required to act as a telltale to the officer of the deck. When braced back, they will begin to lift (luff) before the lower sails and thus will serve as a warning to trim sail or fall off before the ship is caught aback. When braced sharp in light air, the yards are fanned properly when each yard on the weather side can be seen just aft of the one below it when viewed from under the course yard.

As the wind and heel increase, the fan should be progressively increased until there is a difference of approximately a quarter of a point between each yard. Normally, yards are fanned only when the wind is near or forward of the beam. As the wind draws aft, the effects mentioned above become less important and eventually can be ignored. Thus, when the wind is more than a point abaft the beam, the yards are *stacked,* or positioned one right above the other.

SAIL BALANCE

As *Eagle* moves through the water, numerous forces act upon her hull, superstructure, and rigging. Analyzing these forces can be difficult to understand. To explain the basic concepts, we will call a certain point on the ship the pivot point. If the forces acting forward of this point are in equilibrium with those acting aft of it, the ship will move forward in a straight line with no weather helm. The location of this point depends on several factors, including ship's speed, trim, and wetted surface area, but it is usually found just forward of the mainmast. When the center of effort of all the sails set is directly above the center of lateral resistance, the ship will be in balance.

If the ship is not in balance, either weather or lee helm will be present. *Weather helm* occurs when the ship tends to round up into the wind, and *lee helm* occurs when the ship tends to fall off. As you can see in figure 32, the headsails and foresails are forward of the pivot point (PP), the

Fig. 32. Combined center of effort for all sails

Sailing full and by, with proper sail balance
Note: slight weather helm necessary to maintain course.

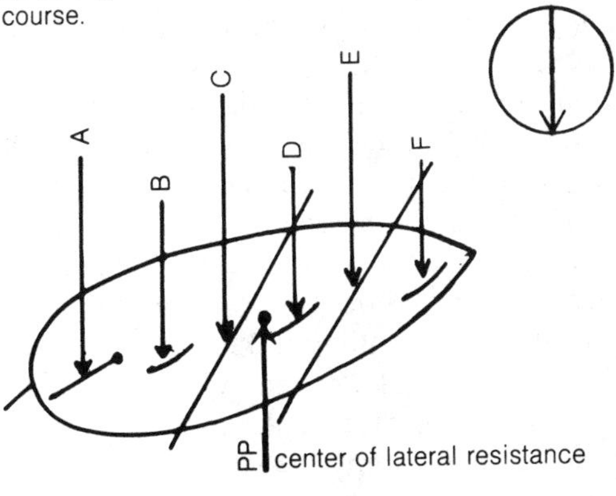

PP center of lateral resistance

main staysails are close to the pivot point, while the remaining sails and the rudder are aft of the point. If the sails set are not balanced carefully, there will be a greater force either forward or aft of the pivot point.

Eagle's rudder is comparably larger than the rudder on most power driven vessels. In addition to turning the ship, it can act as a brake whose effect, because of the resistance of the water, can offset the driving power of several sails. It is beneficial to carry as little rudder as possible while still keeping as many sails set as possible.

In practice most sailing vessels are designed to sail with slight weather helm. This ensures that the ship will luff up into the wind and lose way in the event of a steering casualty or other similar problem. Slight weather helm also maximizes driving power and gives the OOD a better feel of the ship, allowing course changes to be made to compensate for wind shifts without relying solely on the compass or telltales. *Eagle* usually carries about 5 degrees of weather helm when sailing close-hauled. More weather helm can sometimes be carried without losing speed, particularly in a good breeze.

In strong winds, *Eagle* will heel to leeward. Heeling actually slows the vessel and can be dangerous if it becomes excessive. Heeling causes the airflow across the sails to be disturbed, resulting in less driving power. Additionally, the bow will dig in and the keel will present less lateral resistance, resulting in more leeway. Some heeling is acceptable, but the OOD must always be prepared to douse upper sails or fall off to ensure that it does not become excessive.

Sail balance is usually achieved through trimming individual sails. Decisions as to the order and number of sails to be set should be made with sail balance kept in mind. Each sail must be properly trimmed to ensure that the overall sail balance can be achieved.

The spanker is particularly important in sail balance. As one of the largest sails and as the farthest aft, it creates a large turning moment. As a result it sometimes must be eased out beyond its optimum point of sail to eliminate excessive weather helm. This generally occurs in light air. When the wind is on the quarter, it may even be necessary to brail in the spanker. Sometimes it is found that the speed lost by brailing in may be compensated for by the lessening of the need to carry excessive rudder. When excessive weather helm is observed, however, the OOD should not immediately ease the spanker or brail it in. Many times the problem is found in improperly trimmed sails forward of the pivot point (e.g., fore yards not braced sharp or not fanned, headsails sheeted in too far, or excessive cockbill).

BRACING AND COCKBILL

Bracing with Sails Furled

Because of the number of other lines that are affected when the yards are moved, bracing is more complicated than merely hauling on the braces on one side and easing them on the other. In general, the buntlines, leechlines, buntleechlines, and to a lesser extent the sheets and clewlines will become taut on the side of the yard that is to be braced forward (new weather side) and will become slack on the side that is to be braced aft (new lee side). Collectively these lines are called the *lee gear.* If they are not properly handled, lines may part, the bull's eyes and lizards may be pulled out, or the sail may rip. The same effect is experienced by the fixed lifts, and bracing always results in the yards being *cockbilled,* or canted at an angle to the horizon when sails are not set.

The cause of *cockbill* when sails are not set can be seen by examining the case of the fixed lifts in figure 33. The lifts lead from fittings on the sides of the mast to the yardarms (fig. 33C). When a yard is braced (to port in this case), it pivots on a pin on the yard shoe (O). Yards theoretically swing in the horizontal arc (AA′) or (BB′). The fixed lifts, however, pivot at their fittings on the sides of the mast (at C and E) and can swing only in an arc (DD′) or (FF′). Since the lifts of the upper three yards are not adjustable, the yard cannot actually swing in a horizontal arc from A to A′. It is canted upwards, or cockbilled, as the port lift becomes taut (as shown in figure 33B). The opposite yardarm cockbills downward and takes up the slack gained in the starboard lift. This principle is most easily understood by climbing aloft and actually examining the yards when they are in their fixed lifts.

The lifts on the courses are adjustable. It is possible, therefore, to brace these yards without developing cockbill by easing the lift on the side on which the yard is being braced forward (new weather side) and by hauling on the opposite lift (on the same side as the braces that are being hauled). The lower topsail yard has no lifts and

Fig. 33. Bracing with yards in fixed lifts

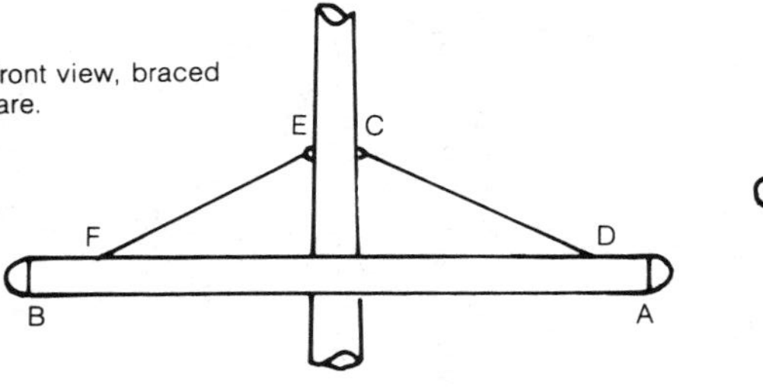

A. Front view, braced square.

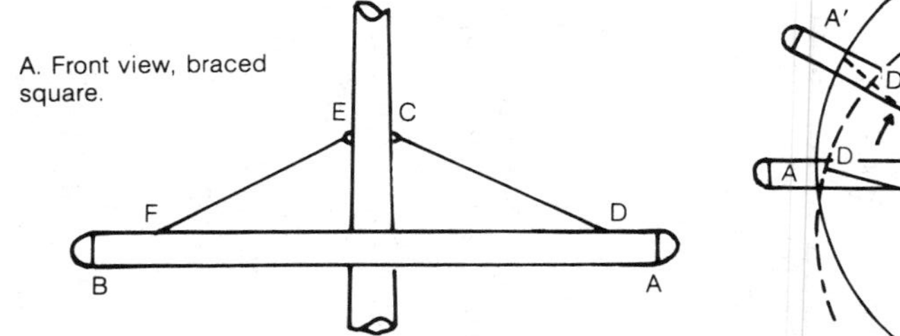

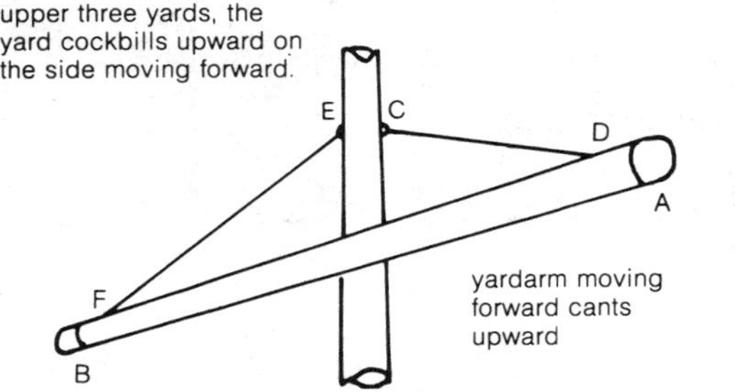

B. Front view, braced on port tack. Since lifts are not adjustable on the upper three yards, the yard cockbills upward on the side moving forward.

C. Top view, bracing toward port tack. The yard pivots at O, forward of the mast but the lifts pivot at C and E on the side of the mast. Since the lifts, except on the courses, are not adjustable, the yardarm must rise on the side that is braced forward (here the port) and drop on the side that moves aft. One lift (CD) comes taut and cants the yard upward and the other lift (EF) becomes slack and allows the yard to cant downward on that side.

will parallel the upper topsail yard if the upper topsail sheets are belayed. Since the courses will not necessarily cockbill, the lower topsail sheets may have to be eased when bracing around.

In actual practice, the yards are kept cockbilled at the same angle when braced sharp with the sails furled, in order to present a neater appearance and to prevent the lower topsail yard from being fouled as the upper topsail yard cockbills. If the course yards are allowed to cockbill, the tack and sheet on the side on which the yard is moving forward (weather side) will grow taut as the yard cockbills upward and must be eased while the opposite tack and sheet must be rounded in. If the yards are not parallel after bracing, the lower topsail yard, which does not have a lift, can most easily be paralleled to the upper topsail yard by adjusting the sheets of the lower and upper topsails. In figure 34, the four sheets form two opposing pairs. The course yards can be adjusted by throwing off the lower topsail sheets and adjusting the lifts.

Just as the lifts are affected by bracing, so too are the buntlines, bunt-leechlines, and leechlines, whose leads are approximately the same as the lifts. As the yardarm moves forward, the lines become taut and may part, pull out lizards or bull's eyes, or tear the sail, especially when the sails are harbor furled. On the opposite side, the lines will hang slack. Thus, in bracing, the lines on the side on which the yardarm is moving forward must be taken off their pin or at least eased. Clewlines and sheets lead along the edge of the yard and pivot fairly close to where the yard itself pivots. As a result, they are less af-

Fig. 34. Procedures for removing cockbill. Sails are not set.

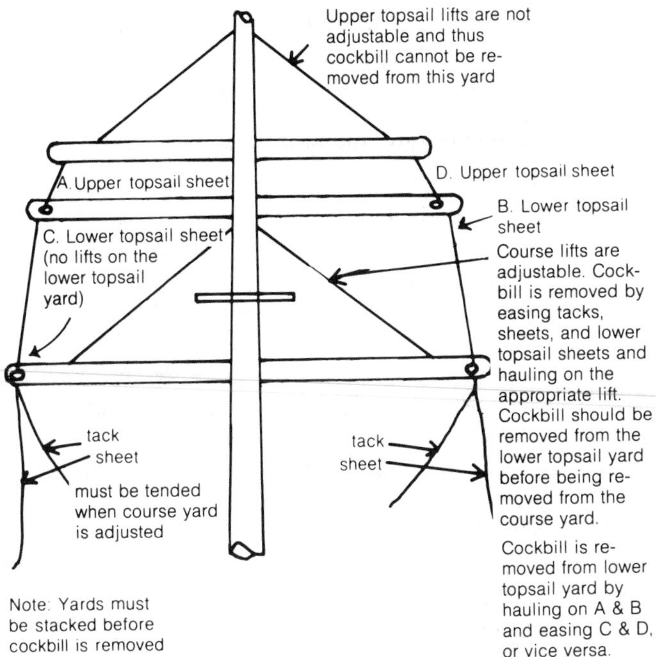

fected by the movement of the yard. Nevertheless, if they are snug before the bracing evolution begins, they will become taut and possibly part on the side on which the yard is moving forward.

Under ideal conditions, as few as ten cadets can successfully brace the yards when the sails are doused, although more are preferable. Individual cadets should be assigned to each of the course tacks and sheets. One cadet can handle all of the braces that are eased, although one for each line is preferred. A bare minimum of three cadets is required on the side to be hauled for each of the course and lower topsail braces, two for the upper topsail, and one each for the topgallant and royal braces.

On the main, the proximity of the braces to the boat davits often causes problems. Unless handled carefully, the braces foul on the after davit. The *timenoguy* is a whip running from the mizzen shrouds to the main brace and is used to haul the brace clear of the davits. It may also be necessary to station a cadet with a special U-shaped boat hook near the davit to keep the brace clear.

The following is the sequence of commands for bracing:

1. Preparatory steps include faking out the appropriate braces, tacks, and sheets for running. All clewlines, buntlines, bunt-leechlines, and leechlines (lee gear) on the side on which the yardarm is to move forward (new weather side) should be taken off their pins. The course lifts should also be taken off the pins.

2. Bracing around:

a. Mast Captain: "*Tend your tacks and sheets. Ease the starboard (port) main braces. Haul around on the port (starboard) main braces.*"

b. Because of the differences in the purchases of the braces and the weights of the yards, the royal and topgallant yards will normally come around faster than the lower three yards. The mast captain usually delegates the responsibility of keeping the yards moving together to the brace captain. The mast captain may give the order, "*Handsomely,*" "*Lively,*" or "*That's well on the main royal (topgallant, etc.) brace,"* if the yards are not being braced together.

c. If bracing square or bracing sharp, the cadets easing the braces should ease them out until they reach their *leather*. The leathers consist of short strips of leather that are inserted into the brace after the braces have been stretched out to mark the proper position for the yard when it is square or braced sharp with a fan.

d. Once the yards are in position, all slack must be taken out of the braces. This must be done before sending cadets aloft or before securing, to keep the yards from moving and possibly damaging gear or causing someone to lose their footing.

Bracing with Sails Set

Bracing the yards with the sails set is similar to bracing with the sails furled. With the upper three yards up, however, the fixed lifts hang slack. As discussed, all of the yards are now joined through the leeches of their sails. Thus it is possible to remove the cockbill from all five yards by adjusting the course lifts. As discussed, the yards should be kept parallel to the horizon to allow the best angle of attack of wind on the sails. When bracing with all sail set, the inertia of the tremendous weight of the gear will often result in the yards cockbilling, even if the course lifts are off their pins. For this reason, it is necessary to haul on the fore and main lifts on the side on which the braces are being hauled so that the yards can be kept parallel to the horizon. While the yards are in motion, several cadets can adjust the lifts; once the yards are braced, many more will be needed to do the same job and tacks, sheets, and other braces will have to be handled. The lift that is hauled to remove cockbill is always the lee lift once the yards have been braced.

The wind usually strikes the sail at such an angle that the weather braces have more strain than the lee braces, so more people will be needed to brace when the sails are set than when they are doused. The extra cadets are assigned proportionately to the lines. If the courses remain set, it is particularly important to have sufficient people on the sheet that will be hauled. It is also important that the cadets assigned to the tack and sheet (which have been eased out) pay particular attention not to let the lines run away and cause severe rope burns.

Similarly, those easing the braces must not lose control and let the yards slam up against the backstays. Not only is this dangerous, but it is a tremendous waste of manpower and time. One or two cadets not paying attention and easing the weather brace too far will result in many cadets being assigned to that brace to haul the yard against the wind and back off the backstays. There is no excuse for yards being braced too far, especially with leathers properly adjusted.

Before bracing from the sharp position, the tack-jigger must be cleared away. The lee gear must again be removed from the pins on the side on which the yardarm will move forward. Sheets should be watched carefully in case they become too taut and jam in the cheek block on the yardarm, although sheets are normally not a problem with sails set.

The commands for bracing with the sails set are the same as those given when the sails are doused, except that the command "*Haul around on the port (starboard) lift*" will be given as appropriate.

Trimming sail on any sailing vessel is an art mastered only by practice. Nevertheless, it is an art that must be mastered. Efficient trimming can make a difference of many miles during a watch. Proper trimming develops a sense of wind and the sea. This sense is indispensable for a seaman on any vessel, sail or power. The wind and the sea are constantly changing and only the alert OOD takes advantage of these changes to continually make adjustments and maximize the speed of the ship.

WORKING THE SHIP ▪ 6

Over the centuries, square-rigger sailors have developed an intimacy with the sea that modern-day seamen find hard to emulate. Those who dedicated their lives to sailing such vessels relied solely on the wind and sea for the success or failure of their voyage. Today, *Eagle* requires the same dedication and skill from those who sail her that is now part of square-rigger folklore. As in days gone by, *Eagle* must use the wind to its best advantage—this chapter focuses on how to best accomplish this.

Under full sail, *Eagle* can point to within about 75 degrees of the true wind. Her fore-and-aft sails alone will carry as close as about 45 degrees. In practice, however, *Eagle* is sailed under fore-and-aft sails alone only when motor-sailing. This is done to gain added speed and to improve stability. Whenever a sailing vessel's destination lies further upwind than she can sail, it is necessary to slowly work up to windward by zigzagging back and forth in a series of *tacks*. Without deviating too far from her intended trackline, the vessel gains as much distance upwind as possible on each leg. Then she will *come about* or tack by putting the wind on the other side, and continue to work upwind until the final destination is reached.

For a square-rigger this is a very long and arduous process. Gaining a single mile upwind will require sailing many miles, tacking numerous times. Realistically, a square-rigger does not sail well upwind and sometimes may actually lose ground. Therefore, proper sail trim and taking advantage of every wind shift is essential when sailing close-hauled. Equally important is the ability to tack or *wear* quickly with a minimum loss of ground.

There are three basic methods of changing tacks: *tacking,* where the bow is brought through the wind; *wearing,* where the stern is brought through; and *boxhauling,* where elements of a tack and wear are combined to allow the ship to come about in a minimum amount of sea room.

Of these three, tacking is the preferred method. Tacking takes less time, loses less ground, and only requires the bow to swing through about 160 degrees. On the other hand, *wearing* is a relatively slow evolution, requires turning through about 200 degrees, and carries the ship downwind throughout the entire evolution, thereby losing valuable ground gained to windward.

When wearing, the staysails are doused and the spanker is brailed in before the evolution begins. Also, the foresails are blanketed by the main square sails for most of the evolution. As a result, wearing takes much longer, usually twenty minutes or more. Wearing is relatively easy to understand, however, and can be safely executed in almost any weather.

Tacking is more difficult, and teamwork and timing are critical. A tack can be accomplished in less than half the time of a wear, however—five to six minutes with a trained crew. If preparation time is included, the advantage of tacking is even more apparent. Most important, however, is that the ship can actually gain distance upwind while tacking, since the turn is made into the wind and not downwind. Since all sails remain set while preparing for the evolution, even more ground is gained and ship speed is maintained longer than when wearing.

There are situations, however, where the ship cannot or should not tack. In tacking, the fore square sails are brought aback where they act as a huge brake. In light winds the ship may not have enough way to overcome this braking effect. In higher winds it may be dangerous to put the square sails aback. This danger becomes quite evident if you recall *Eagle*'s mast support as described in chapter 2. The masts are supported primarily by shrouds and backstays that oppose the wind force on the after side of the sails. Only a few stays, however, have a forward lead to support the masts when the sails are aback.

In general, *Eagle* should not be tacked when the true wind speed exceeds about 25 knots, because of the danger to the rig (making over 12 knots through the water). Also, *Eagle* will usually not tack in winds of less than 10 knots, because she will not have enough speed to make it through the wind (when making less than 5 knots through the water).

These speeds provide only a rough rule of thumb. In flat, calm seas the ship may tack when sailing in winds of less than 10 knots and in heavier seas she may miss stays in winds of 15 knots or more. Finally, tacking is an evolution that requires all hands on deck. If only a small number of cadets are available, as in a normal watch section, it is necessary to wear rather than tack.

Boxhauling is used when it is necessary to come about in a minimum of space, as in a crowded harbor or confined channel. It combines the elements of a tack and a wear. The ship first turns upwind, is caught aback, then falls off onto the original tack and finally wears around onto the new tack. Boxhauling may also be used to recover from an unsuccessful tack, where the ship has come dead in the water before coming through the wind.

TACKING

A successful tack requires careful preparation, teamwork, and execution, and an understanding of the forces affecting the ship. When *Eagle* tacks, all hands are on deck and cadets face one of their greatest challenges at sea. The upperclass must be organized and establish a clear chain of command; they must not only memorize the commands but also develop an understanding of the forces and basic principles involved. The cadet OOD will give the commands and is in control of the evolution. A forehanded OOD will develop a thorough understanding of this chapter before assuming the watch. The three cadet mast captains will carry out the orders of the cadet OOD at their respective masts.

For a successful tack, a square-rigger must be sailing *full and by*. The ship should be sailed as close to the wind as possible, to minimize the distance she has to turn through the wind. On the other hand, the vessel must be sailed off the wind far enough that the best possible speed is maintained to ensure that the bow will go through.

Additionally, the sails should be handled to help rather than hinder the swing of the ship. The headsails and spanker are the farthest from the pivot point; in addition to driving the ship forward they also impart a turning moment about the pivot point that can be used to help bring the ship through the wind. These will be important sails to handle during the tack.

Eagle, like most sailing vessels, carries slight weather helm whenever she is sailing close-hauled. Therefore, with all sails set, the ship naturally wants to turn into the wind. This natural force should be taken advantage of when coming about. It has been found that slowly applying a moderate amount of rudder (10 to 15 degrees) is more than adequate to bring the bow through the wind and onto the new tack. While it may seem that full rudder would be most effective, this is often not the case, since the rudder can act as a brake, particularly in light air.

By far, the most important element in the tack is for the cadet officer of the deck to ensure that *Eagle* is sailing *on the wind* and that all sails are properly trimmed before the evolution begins. *Pinching* or sailing *off the wind* is frequently the cause of missing stays. Regardless of how the sails are handled or the timing of the commands, if *Eagle* is not sailing close to the wind with all sails drawing properly, she may not make it through the wind.

Mast captains are responsible for trimming sails on their mast before reporting "*manned and ready*." For the square sails, yards are fanned, cockbill removed, weather leeches are taut, and all gear is overhauled. All sheets on the fore-and-aft sails are properly trimmed and scallops are removed along the luffs.

Before tacking, all necessary gear must be carefully faked out. A jammed brace, for example, can cause the ship to miss stays. A jammed halyard may result in a torn sail. To prevent such a mishap, staysail halyards and sheets, as well as the lee braces, must be faked out for running. Buntlines, bunt-leechlines, leechlines, and clewlines must be taken off their pins on the lee side to prevent them from coming taut and parting as the yards are braced. The tack-jiggers are usually cleared away. The foresail, however, provides significant driving power and balances the turning force of the spanker. Thus, in marginal tacking conditions, the tack-jigger should remain boarded until just before the command

"*Let go and haul.*" All sails are properly trimmed and the ship should be sailing *full and by*.

When all masts report "manned and ready," the informational command "*helm's alee*" is given. The spanker boom is hauled amidships and the rudder command is given to start the turn upwind. Hauling the spanker boom amidships helps force the stern downwind and allows the spanker to continue to draw as the bow turns up into the wind.

If trimmed properly, the headsails will luff as soon as the ship starts the turn upwind. They should be watched closely to ensure that they do not slat about, but they should not be sheeted flat, which would hinder the swing of the ship. The remaining sails are kept drawing to drive the ship forward. Sometimes the mizzen staysails are sheeted slightly flatter than normal to allow them to carry longer, to keep them driving forward and to help swing the stern downwind.

As the ship turns into the wind, the square sails will eventually start to lift (luff) and will become ineffective. At this point the mainsail is brought up into its gear. This is done for three reasons. First, if left set, the mainsail would quickly back and would act as a huge brake since it is the largest sail (same size as foresail). In addition, the leads of the mainsail sheets and tacks are extremely long, so it is very difficult to handle them when bracing and these cadets can be used more effectively elsewhere. Finally, by bringing the mainsail up into its gear, the OOD has a clear view forward and can more easily control the evolution. With an untrained or reduced crew, the mainsail is sometimes brought up into its gear before the evolution begins to ensure that there are enough hands to execute the command "*Mainsail haul.*"

While the mainsail is being hauled up into its gear, the main staysails are being doused. These sails may still be filling but not to their best advantage, and since they will soon be luffing, they can easily be spared. It is easier to douse them when they are slightly filled than when they are luffing violently. This enables a small number of cadets to shift their sheets to the new tack and to have them ready to reset by the time the ship is through the wind, reducing the overall time for completion of the maneuver. Most importantly, the cadets are available and within a short time will be hauling on the braces. The mizzen staysails, on the other hand, are held as long as they will fill. This provides additional drive as well as a force aft of the pivot point.

As the ship continues to turn, the upper square sails on the main will begin to back. Then, the command "*Mainsail haul*" is given, and the main yards are hauled around to the new tack. This action—the most critical of the entire evolution—requires precise timing. Otherwise, the ship may not make it through the wind. If the yards are hauled around too soon, much of the main sail area, which would otherwise be blanketed by the fore, will be fully exposed to the wind and act as a brake (fig. 35).

If the yards are hauled around too late, the main square sails will back along their entire width and a tremendous amount of manpower will be needed to haul the braces. This causes the yards to be braced more slowly, resulting in a decrease in speed or *Eagle* gaining sternway.

The proper time for the command is when the weather leeches of the main square sails begin to back. Bracing at this time allows the wind to do most of the work, forcing the yards around quickly, since most of the mainmast sail area is blanketed by the fore. If timed correctly, only a minimum amount of effort is needed once the yards begin moving onto their new tack.

The lee braces are eased rapidly out to their leathers while the weather braces are hauled. The yards must be kept under control and must not run past their leathers, to prevent them from slamming up against the backstays and causing damage. As the yards move, there may be slack in the lee braces and sometimes even in the weather braces. To prevent fouling of the main brace on the boat davits, a cadet should be ready to man the timenoguy to haul the main brace clear.

As the bow comes through the wind, the headsail sheets are shifted onto the new tack. If the ship has come dead in the water, they may be backed on the original tack to increase their turning effect. The spanker is eased so that it does not force the stern downwind, and the rudder is put amidships.

The ship will continue to swing onto the new tack. When the mainsails begin to draw, the command "*Let go and haul*" is given, and the foreyards are braced onto the new tack. As soon as possible, the main and the mizzen staysails are reset and then the mainsail. Unless otherwise ordered, all sails set on the old tack are reset on the

Fig. 35. Timing for mainsail haul

A. Given too soon, the main sails back and act as a brake, stopping the ship.

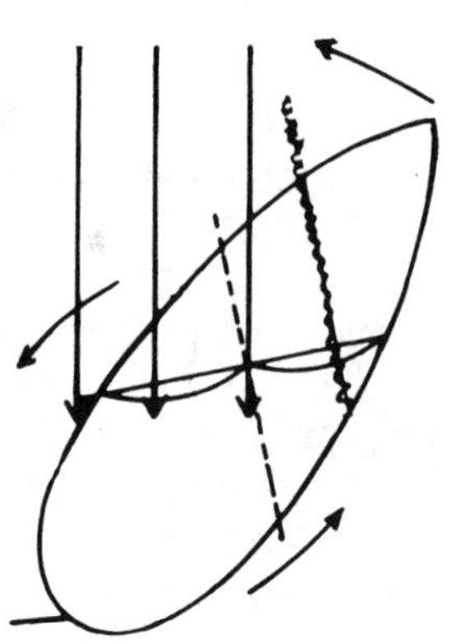

B. Given too late, the main sails are blanketed by the fore. Wind passing under the foresails backs mainsails along their entire width. Extra effort is needed to brace the yards.

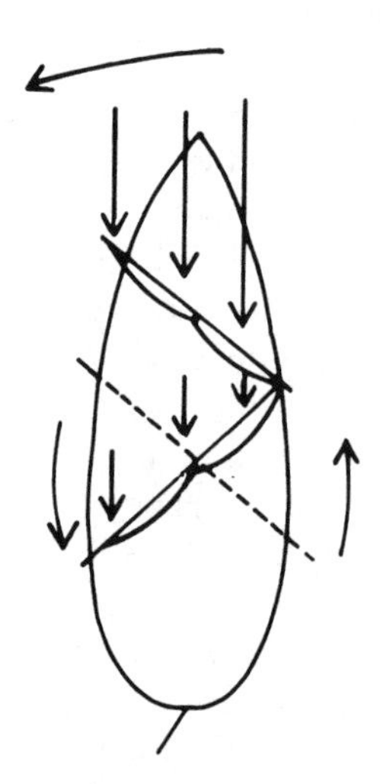

C. Given at the proper time, the wind backs only the weather edge of the mainsails and forces the yards around. Only the wind passing under the foresails strikes the lee side of the mainsails.

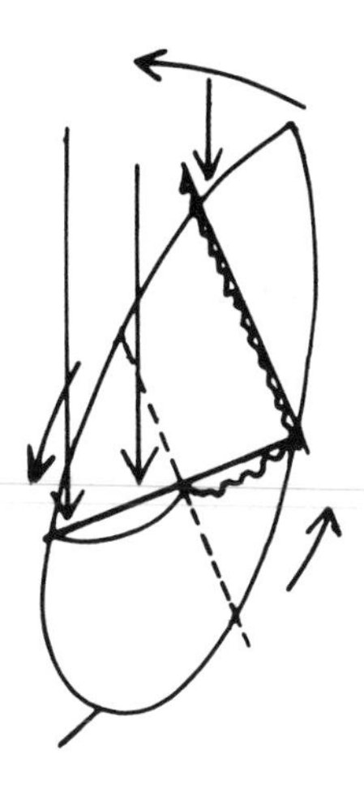

new; if the tack was boarded on the old tack, it will be boarded on the new. All sails are trimmed to their best advantage without further order.

At times the ship will come dead in the water while she is head to wind. *Eagle* will then gain sternway very rapidly and the rudder must be shifted to allow the bow to swing onto the new tack. With the fore square sails aback, the ship can usually gain enough sternway to back around onto the new tack. Occasionally, the ship will not properly answer her helm in such conditions. She is then said to be *in irons*.

In such circumstances it may be beneficial to brail in the spanker, to eliminate its tendency to keep the bow into the wind. If the ship falls off onto the original tack, the main yards must be rebraced, the staysails reset, and the speed built up to attempt another tack. If time is of the essence, it may be better to consider the unsuccessful tack as the first part of a boxhaul.

Organization and teamwork are critically important in tacking. Throughout the age of sail, crews of twenty or less routinely tacked vessels much larger than *Eagle*. The large complement of cadets on board *Eagle* allows a tack to be accomplished more expeditiously and with less individual effort. It requires closer supervision, however, because of the relative inexperience of the underclass cadets and because a single brace or halyard improperly faked out or untended may cause the ship to miss stays. Although the division of effort among the cadets is subject to variation, the following organization has proved effective.

The foremast personnel should initially man the main staysail downhauls and prepare for bracing. The foremast personnel are free during the first half of a tack and handle the main staysail downhauls, because the mainmast cadets will be busy handling the staysails and mainsail and laying aft to haul the main braces. As soon as the main staysails are doused, the cadets on the fore can lay to their braces, foresail tacks, and sheets and can stand by to brace the foreyards.

The tack-jigger must be cleared away on the courses before bracing can begin. Since the foresail is a large driving sail, however, the tack-jigger should not be cleared away too early or the loss of driving power may result in missed stays. The foresail is also important in sail balance and offsets the force aft of the spanker. If the tack-jigger is cleared away too early, excess weather helm may result in addition to the loss of driving power.

The mainmast personnel should man the mainsail gear, the staysail halyards, and the sheets for the main staysails. The cadets assigned to the mainsail tacks and sheets should remain at their stations because the yards will be braced almost immediately after the mainsail has been taken in. The on-watch Ready Boat Crew should help man the main braces. If the yards are hauled at the right time, the wind will do most of the work.

After the mainsail has been taken in, the cadets assigned should lay back to the braces to assist with "mainsail haul." In a good breeze, the command "*Mainsail haul*" is given almost simultaneously with "*Rise tacks and sheets*." Thus, careful stationing of personnel is essential if mainmast personnel are to be ready to respond to both commands when directed. The mainsail is not reset until the staysails have been reset, all yards have been properly fanned, and cockbill taken out for the new tack.

Normally, a single cadet is assigned to each of the staysail halyards, two to each sheet, and one to each of the mainsail tacks and sheets. An upperclass cadet and two or three underclass cadets should be assigned to shift the staysail sheets once the staysails have been doused. Working steadily, they can have all of the sails ready to be reset by the time the bow has passed through the wind. One cadet is stationed in the tops before the evolution begins to stand by to shift the staysail sheet pendants.

Mizzen personnel should man the mizzen staysail gear, the spanker sheet, vangs, preventer, and flag halyards. The spanker is hauled against the wind, so as many cadets as possible should be stationed on the spanker sheet. Hauling the spanker boom also requires cadets to ease the preventer and tend the vangs and flag halyards. Once this is accomplished these cadets should assist with the mizzen staysail downhauls.

The commands for tacking are shown in figure 36:

1. Preparatory steps:

a. Cadet OOD: "*All hands to sail stations*."

b. Mast captains: "*Fore (main, mizzen) manned*" (when enough cadets are at the mast to handle sail).

c. Cadet OOD: "*Ready about*." This command means, "Prepare to tack."

d. Mast captains: "*Fore (main, mizzen) manned and ready*." This report should not be given until all lines that will run have been faked out; all lee clewlines, buntlines, bunt-leechlines, and leechlines have been taken off their pins; all lines are manned; and everyone is ready to start the evolution.

2. Bringing ship into the wind:

a. Cadet OOD: "*Helm's alee*." This is an informational command notifying all personnel that the maneuver has begun.

b. Cadet OOD to mizzenmast captain: "*Haul the spanker boom amidships*."

c. Cadet OOD to helmsman: "*Right (Left) rudder*." The rudder command is normally given as the spanker boom begins moving amidships. If

Fig. 36. Tacking

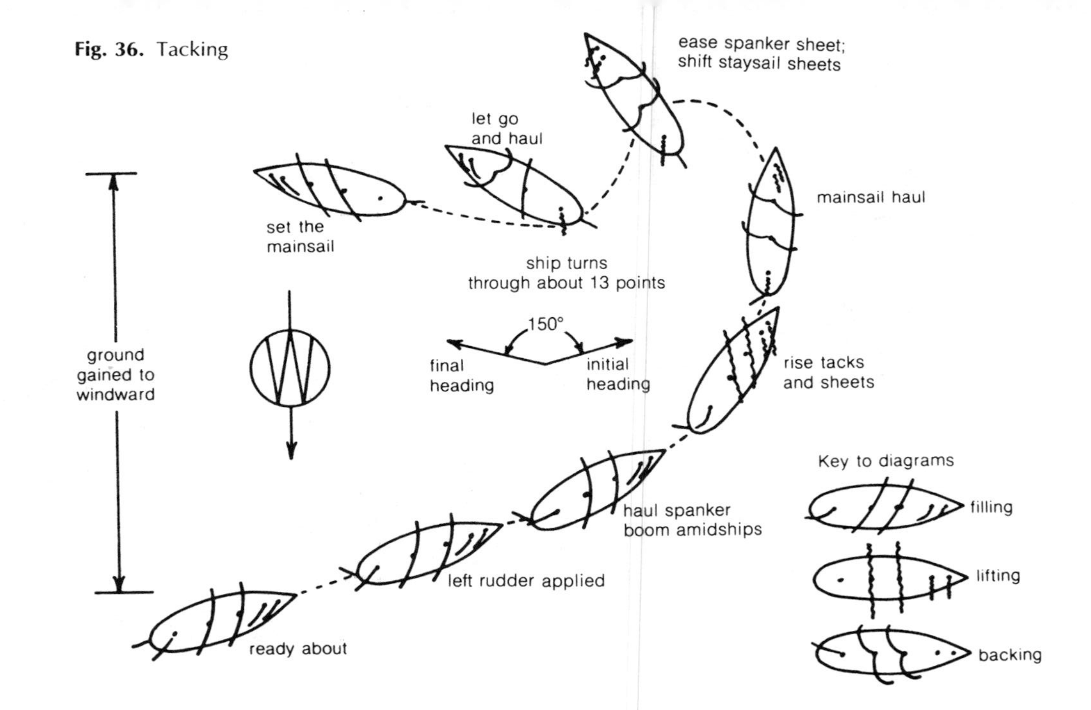

timed correctly, the spanker will continue to drive the ship forward as the turn upwind is made, and it also will provide a turning moment.

3. Bracing the main:

a. Cadet OOD to main and mizzenmast captains: "*Rise tacks and sheets.*" This command is given when the weather leeches of the main square sails begin to lift. On this command the mainmast captain takes in the mainsail and douses the main staysails, and the mizzenmast captain douses the mizzen staysails. There is no separate command from the cadet OOD concerning the staysails. As discussed earlier, the mizzenmast captain usually holds the mizzen staysails as long as possible to take advantage of their driving power and turning effect. The mizzen staysails must be kept under control at all times to keep from endangering bridge personnel.

b. Cadet OOD to mainmast captain: "*Mainsail haul.*" This command should be given as soon as the weather leeches of the main square sails begin to back.

4. Head to the wind:

a. Cadet OOD to foremast captain: "*Shift the headsail sheets,*" or, if the vessel has lost headway and may not come through the wind, "*Lead aft the lee sheets,*" in which case the headsails are reset flat on the old tack so that they will back and help swing the bow off onto the new tack.

b. Cadet OOD to mizzenmast captain: "*Ease the spanker.*" The spanker is eased out as far as necessary so that it will not hold the bow up into the wind.

c. The cadet OOD should give orders to the

helm as appropriate. If the ship's head comes through the wind, the rudder should be eased to prevent the vessel from swinging too far off the wind on the new tack and losing ground downwind. If the ship comes dead in the water and then gains sternway, the rudder should be shifted to back the ship around onto the new tack.

5. On the new tack:

a. Cadet OOD to foremast captain: "*Let go and haul.*" This command is given when the mainsails begin to fill. The foreyards are braced quickly around to the new tack. Note: if the command "*Mainsail haul*" is slow to be executed, the command "*Let go and haul*" should be given as soon as the bow has passed well through the wind. Waiting for the main to be braced in this case simply results in added leeway and more time until the ship regains headway.

b. Cadet OOD to main and mizzenmast captains: "*Set the mainsail.*" On this command, first the main and mizzen staysails are reset and then the mainsail. No further commands are needed from the cadet OOD.

c. After all sails are set, each mast captain trims sail and fans the yards appropriately for the new tack. When braced sharp, the fore and main yards should be fanned unless the cadet OOD directs otherwise.

WEARING

Wearing with a Full Crew

Compared to tacking, wearing is a leisurely evolution that can be carried out even by the Ready Boat Crew. It has the disadvantages of being time-consuming and losing valuable distance gained to windward. Nevertheless, wearing may be necessary in very strong or light winds and where not enough hands are available for a tack.

In wearing, the turn is downwind versus upwind, a procedure opposite that of tacking. As in tacking, the sails are used to their best advantage to assist the ship in turning. Since *Eagle* will not lose headway throughout the entire evolution, however, the rudder is used to do most of the turning and sail balance is less critical than when tacking. Initially, the gaff topsail and staysails are doused and the spanker is brailed in. This eliminates most of the force aft of the pivot point that would otherwise tend to keep the bow into the wind.

More importantly, the main and mizzen staysails must be doused to shift their sheets to the new tack. The mainsail is taken in to facilitate bracing the main and to let wind through to the foresails when the ship turns downwind. As the ship turns downwind, the yards are braced perpendicular to the wind and are kept ***square to the wind*** until they are sharp on the new tack. As the stern passes through the wind, the headsail sheets are shifted and the spanker is set on the new tack. The headsails are trimmed for the new tack. The staysails and mainsail are reset as soon as the yards have been braced sharp and all sails are trimmed for the new tack.

The organization and preparation for wearing are quite simple. The spanker is brailed in and the staysails are all doused before beginning the wear. As in tacking, the lee buntlines, buntleechlines, leechlines, and clewlines should be taken off their pins. All gear that is to run should be carefully faked out.

A few cadets can be broken off to shift the sheets on the main and mizzen staysails while the remainder should man the braces. A single cadet is required for each mainsail tack and sheet unless the wind is strong. About four or five cadets will be needed for each new lee lift. The number of cadets needed for the foresail sheets varies with the wind conditions but normally does not exceed four or five each. The on-watch Ready Boat Crew should assist with the main braces. During the entire evolution, mizzen personnel are engaged in hauling the spanker boom to the new tack, rigging the preventer, and shifting the sheets for the mizzen staysails.

The commands for wearing are shown in figure 37:

1. Preparatory stage:

a. Cadet OOD: "*All hands to sail stations.*"

b. Mast captains: "*Fore (main, mizzen) manned*" (when enough cadets are at the mast to handle sail).

c. Cadet OOD: "*Stand by to wear ship.*" This command is informational and indicates that the ship is about to wear.

d. Mast captain: "*Manned and ready.*" To be manned and ready for a wear, all lee gear is taken off the pins and the lee braces are faked out for running. Foremast personnel should man the headsail sheets and the fore braces, tacks, and sheets. Mainmast personnel must douse the main staysails and then man the mainsail gear and

Fig. 37. Wearing ship: simultaneous bracing

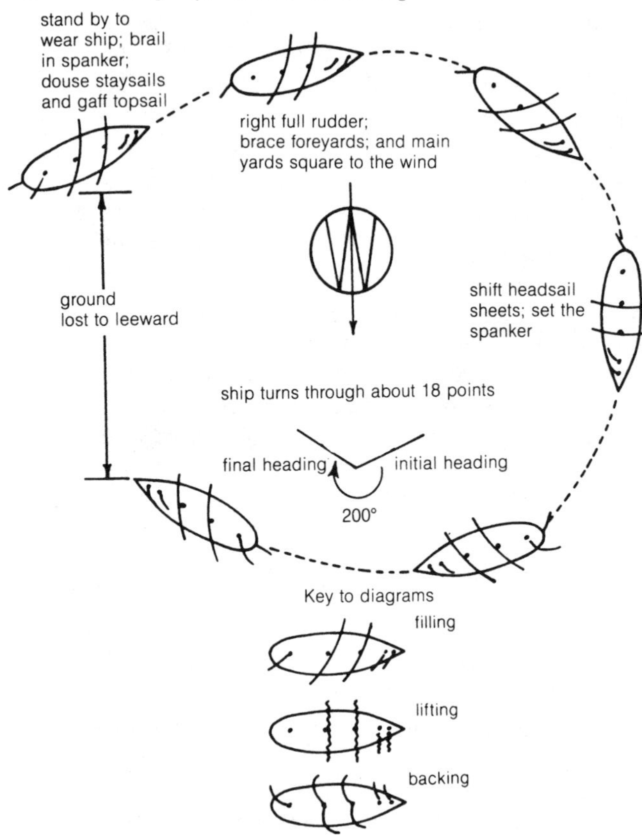

main braces before reporting manned and ready. Mizzen personnel must douse the mizzen staysails, brail in the spanker, and haul the boom onto the new tack before reporting. The tack-jiggers should be cleared away before reporting manned and ready.

e. Cadet OOD to mainmast captain: "*Rise*

tacks and sheets." The mainsail is taken in for three reasons: the leads of the tacks and sheets are long and make the mainsail difficult to handle when the yards are braced; taking in the sail gives the OOD a clear view of the entire ship; and, most importantly, wind is allowed to flow through to the foresails when the ship has turned downwind.

2. Turning off the wind:

a. Cadet OOD: "*Wear-O.*" This command is informational, indicating that the wear has begun.

b. Cadet OOD: "*Left (right) full rudder. Brace the yards* ***square to the wind.***" As the ship begins to turn, the fore and mainmast captains give commands to brace the yards to keep them drawing at their best advantage—*square to the wind.* The ship usually turns slowly, so the actual bracing is done in stages.

Because of the differences in the purchases of the braces, and the different weights of the yards, the topgallant and royal yards tend to get ahead of the lower yards and should be watched carefully. The brace captains should be aware of this and ensure that commands are given to keep the yards moving together. Bracing too far will require much more work at the end of the evolution, because the yards will then have to be hauled against the force of the wind. Mast captains use telltales on their respective masts to keep the yards square to the wind since the relative wind may be slightly different on each mast.

3. Passing through the wind:

a. Cadet OOD to foremast captain: "*Shift the headsail sheets.*" The sheets are shifted to the new tack and trimmed to best advantage as the ship turns back upwind.

b. Cadet OOD to mizzenmast captain: "*Set the spanker.*" Once set, the spanker accelerates the turn of the ship up onto the new course. The spanker does not have to be set, although the turn upwind may take longer without it.

4. Reaching the new course:

a. Cadet OOD: "*Set the mainsail.*" This command is given as soon as the yards have been braced around to the new tack and sails are filling properly. As in tacking, this command directs the mast captains to reset the main and mizzen staysails first and then the mainsail.

b. As soon as the ship reaches her new course, the mast captains should trim their sails and fan their yards properly without further command.

Wearing with a Reduced Crew (Progressive Wear)

When wearing with a watch section, the procedures are basically the same as when wearing with the full crew, except that the yards are braced progressively (fig. 38). The main yards are hauled around until the square sails lift. The sails continue to lift until the yards are braced sharp. This is done so that the force of the wind will not impede the bracing, since so few people are available for bracing. At the same time, the cadet OOD gives the rudder command and turns downwind while the main yards are being braced.

In a progressive wear, the yards are braced ***to the wind,*** while with a full crew they are braced *square to the wind*. The yards are braced so that they parallel the wind and the sails lift but do not

Fig. 38. Wearing ship: progressive bracing

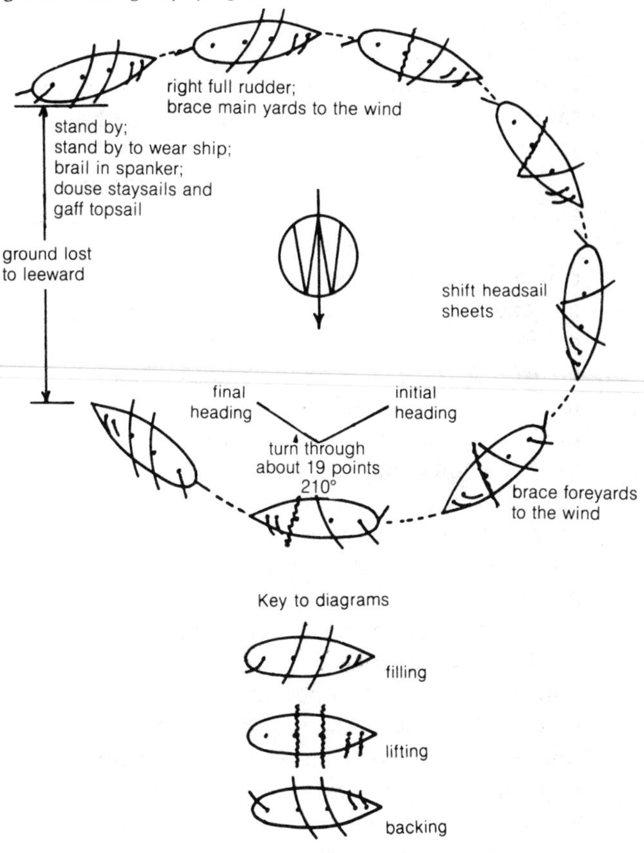

back. It is important not to brace the main around too quickly, for the sails may be caught aback, in which case the ship will quickly lose headway. After the main is braced, the same procedure is used for the fore. As with the main, the fore square sails should lift until they are braced sharp on the new tack.

Both bracing operations require careful coordination between the cadet OOD and the cadet boatswain's mate of the watch. An alert OOD can help start the bracing operation by *pinching* and causing the square sails to lift. If this is done before giving the order "*Brace the main yards* ***to the wind***," the cadets on the braces will not have to haul against the full force of the wind to start the bracing process. As the yards begin to move, the helm command is given, allowing the ship to fall off slowly and turn downwind.

With a small watch section, the maneuver is time-consuming, sometimes lasting an entire watch. It is usually necessary to turn downwind very slowly and then run before the wind so that the headsail sheets can be shifted and the fore braces can be manned before continuing the turn onto the new tack. The spanker can be set when running downwind or this can wait until after the staysails have been reset on the new tack. A progressive wear should be attempted only when speed and distance are not important considerations. If necessary, the evolution can be completed faster by bracing at the change of the watch, using the Ready Boat Crews from both the offgoing and oncoming watch sections.

The commands for a progressive wear are exactly the same as for a simultaneous wear, with one exception. The cadet OOD, instead of ordering "*Brace the yards square to the wind,*" will order "*Brace the main yards* ***to the wind.***" At this command the yards are hauled until the square sails lift, and they continue to lift as the ship turns. When the main has been braced onto the new tack and the ship is running downwind, the command "*Brace the fore yards* ***to the wind***" is given. The fore is brought around until it is sharp on the new tack. The commands for resetting the staysails are then given. It is not necessary to set the spanker, gaff topsail, or mainsail until all other sails are set.

BOXHAULING

Boxhauling is used in crowded anchorages, narrow channels, and other confined waters (fig. 39). Areas such as these make it impossible to *headreach* as far as would be required in tacking but where the loss of ground in wearing is unacceptable. The evolution combines a tack and a wear and is more involved and time-consuming than either.

The first part of the maneuver is exactly like a tack. The spanker boom is hauled amidships and the rudder is put over to turn the ship rapidly up into the wind. When the main square sails begin to lift, the command "*Rise tacks and sheets*" is given and, as in tacking, the main and mizzen staysails are doused. Unlike tacking, the spanker is brailed in because it is being blanketed by the mainsails and will not be needed in the second half of the evolution. Before the bow comes completely into the wind, the command "*Let go and haul*" is given rather than "*Mainsail haul,*" and the foreyards are boxed. When boxed, they rapidly brake the ship. Because they are braced onto

Fig. 39. Situation requiring a boxhaul working up a river

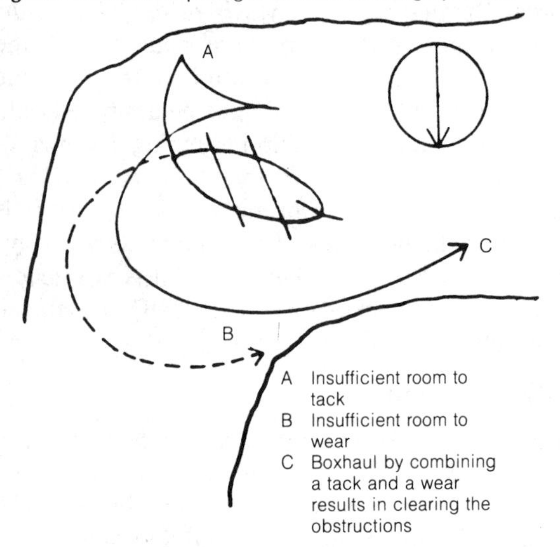

the opposite tack, they tend to force the bow back onto the original tack. The ship gains sternway very rapidly and will swing back onto the original tack. As the ship swings, it may be desirable to brace the main yards to the wind so that they do not draw and oppose the backing effect of the fore.

The second part of the evolution begins when the wind has drawn abeam. Both the fore and main are braced so that they fill. As the ship sails ahead, a normal wear is conducted either by bracing simultaneously or, as in figure 40, progressively. If done correctly, the distance gained upwind during the tacking portion of the maneuver offsets most of the distance normally lost in a wear, so that the ship should end up near where she began—but on the opposite tack.

Fig. 40. Boxhauling

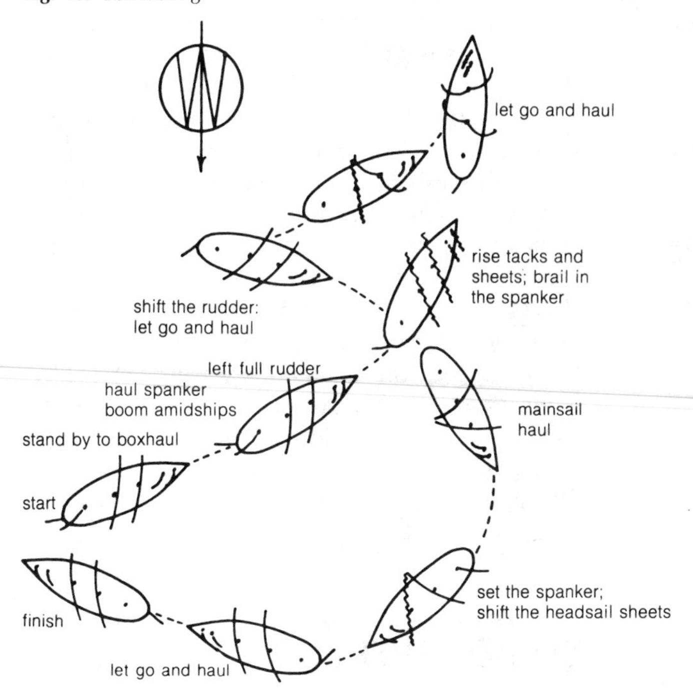

Key to diagrams:

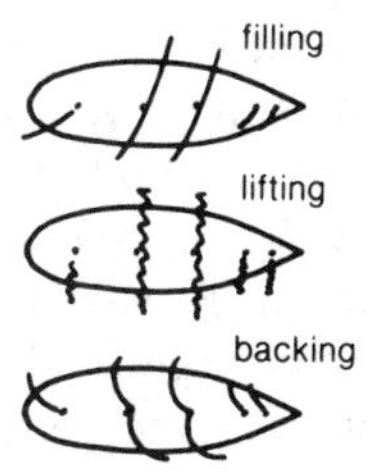

Eagle is rarely required to boxhaul in confined waters since she has an auxiliary engine available for maneuvering in tight situations. Some of these principles, however, may be put to good use when the ship misses stays while attempting to tack. If the ship comes dead in the water after the main yards have been hauled, the fore and main yards will be boxed. The ship will quickly gather sternway. The rudder is shifted and the spanker eased or brailed in. Then the headsail sheets are led aft onto the original tack to help force the bow through. The ship should back into the wind with the main square sails eventually filling on the new tack. The command "Let go and haul" is given and the headsail sheets are shifted after the bow has come through the wind. The ship will gather headway and then be sailing on the new tack.

7 ▪ SHIPBOARD EMERGENCIES

"It appears to me that when an officer takes charge of the deck, his whole mind ought to be occupied with what he would do with the ship in any case of emergency that might take place with the sails that the ship is then under," wrote Captain Learclet of the Royal Navy in 1849. What was true during the Age of Sail remains no less true today. When an emergency strikes, there is rarely enough time to think out a course of action. Forehandedness and training are absolutely essential for any deck officer or cadet in a supervisory position. By anticipating possible emergencies, the officers in charge can avoid most of them and can usually handle the remainder quickly and safely. The sea and wind are ever changing and therefore the proper reaction to any emergency will vary with the circumstances. The officer of the deck must be prepared for an emergency at any time.

CAUGHT ABACK

Perhaps the most common sail emergency is being caught aback. This occurs when the square sails back because of a sudden shift of the wind or the inattention of the helmsman or watch officer. In light air, *Eagle* turns so slowly that it may be impossible to prevent being caught aback by a wind shift. Fortunately, being caught aback in such circumstances is usually more embarrassing than dangerous. In high winds, however, being caught aback can easily result in torn sails, and in extreme conditions, it can cause damage to the yards and rigging. Because the ship will rapidly lose headway with the sails backing, speed is essential to recovery. Because of this loss of headway, much of the recovery action will depend on the proper handling of the sails.

Wind on the Original Tack to Dead Ahead

The first step in all recovery maneuvers, unless the wind has shifted so far as to make it obvious that the procedure will not work, is to put the rudder over and *fall off* (fig. 41).

If the ship comes dead in the water before the sails refill, the foreyards should be boxed so that the increased force of the wind backing the fore forces the bow down (fig. 42A). The spanker should be brailed in, and if the ship gains sternway, the rudder must be shifted. When the ship has fallen off enough for the mainsails to fill, the foreyards are braced again and the ship gathers headway. If the ship turns slowly, it may also be necessary to douse the mizzen staysails to reduce their force aft of the pivot point.

Wind on the Opposite Bow

If the wind has shifted to the original lee bow, and if full rudder has not been successful in bringing the ship around, sail stations will have to be set.

If the wind has shifted to the opposite bow, the ship has, in essence, tacked unintentionally. If there is no objection to sailing on the new tack, the ship recovers by hauling the braces as in a normal tack. Tacks and sheets on the mainsail are risen and staysails are doused as soon as possible. On the fore, the headsail sheets are eased or shifted appropriately. The command "*Mainsail haul*" is given and the foreyards are left on the old tack to help swing the bow off onto the

Fig. 41. Recovering by turning away from wind

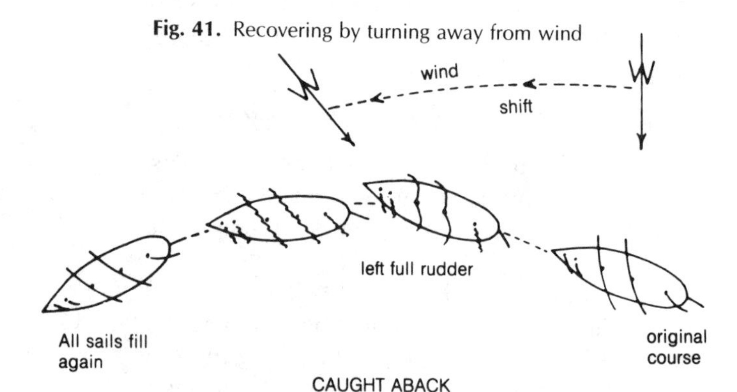

Fig. 42. Recovery from wind shift

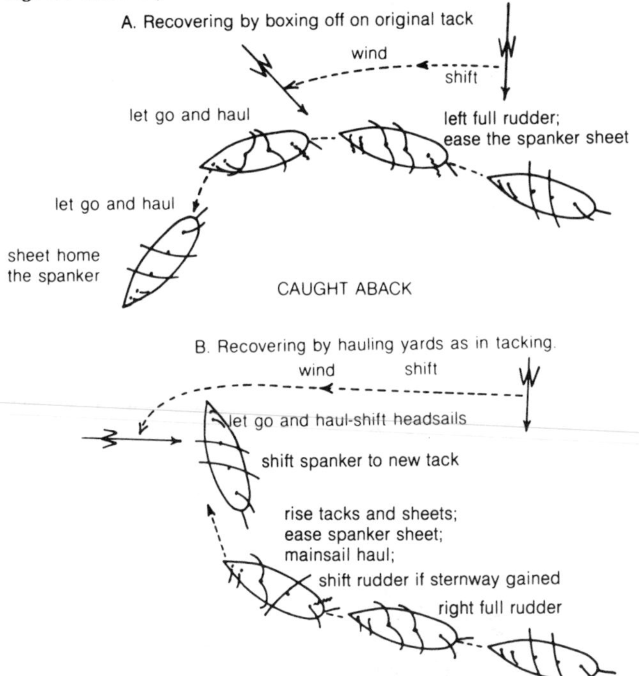

new tack. When the mainsails begin to fill, the command "*Let go and haul*" is given. As the ship starts to gather headway, the mainsail, staysails, and spanker are set and trimmed for the new tack (fig. 42B).

If for some reason it is necessary to sail on the original tack, the ship may be *chapelled* (fig. 43). In chapelling, the main yards are braced square, the spanker is brailed in, and the mainsail and staysails are taken in. The fore, being braced sharp, forces the bow down to leeward on the new tack as do the headsails, whose sheets

Fig. 43. Recovering by chapelling

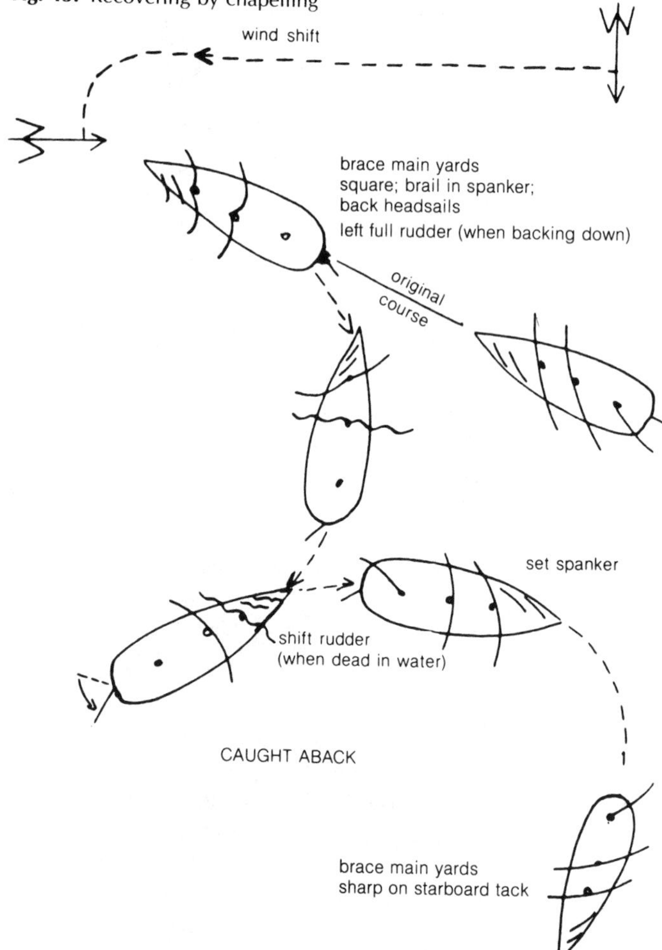

should be held so that they back. As the main is squared, *Eagle* will quickly build up sternway. As she gains sternway, the rudder is shifted and the ship swings her stern up into the wind. The mainsails eventually lift and fill, offsetting the backing power of the fore. As the ship begins to move forward, the rudder is shifted and *Eagle* is wore around onto the original tack, the main being braced to best advantage as the ship turns. The headsail sheets are shifted as the bow passes downwind, and the staysails and spanker are then set.

In chapelling it is particularly important to brail in the spanker first to prevent it from holding the bow up into the wind. Once this is done, the ship will come around, although more slowly, even if the main has not been braced square.

As should be evident, chapelling is very similar to boxhauling with the exception that the yards start off on the opposite tack. In boxhauling, where the purpose is to come about in the least amount of space, the foreyards are braced when falling off and when wearing, to increase the swing of the ship. Since all three masts are worked, the full crew is needed. By contrast, in chapelling the object is merely to recover on the original tack. Thus, it is sufficient to brail in the spanker and, if desired, square the main yards to the ship. This can be done, though with some difficulty, by the Ready Boat Crew.

HEAVY WEATHER SAILING

Shortening Sail

Sailing in heavy weather is not in itself dangerous, but it can be if the watch on deck is not forehanded in anticipating possible problems. For this reason, it is included in this chapter.

There is sometimes a tendency to keep sails set too long when the weather deteriorates (and, conversely, not to reset them soon enough when the weather improves). In actuality, once the ship's heel exceeds 12 to 15 degrees, the increase of the wetted surface and the additional drag offset much of the extra drive of the wind. In particular, the royals and topgallants will do more to heel the ship than to drive her. With excessive heel, the yards will cockbill beyond the point where the lifts can adjust for the heel, resulting in loss of drive.

Excessive heel may also be dangerous since sudden gusts may heel the ship to the point of endangering the vessel. Additionally, the rudder creates more drag as the ship heels further over, at the same time providing less control. In such instances, it is often found that taking in the royals and topgallants and dousing the upper staysails have little or no effect on the speed of the ship, but it is safer and does improve the ride considerably. All in all, the decision to take in sail must depend on several factors, including the amount of sea room available, the condition and forecasted condition of the wind and seas, and the experience level of the crew.

The order of taking in square sails is: royals, topgallants, courses, upper topsails, and lower topsails. In heavy weather, sails are normally taken in and furled one at a time. If they are allowed to slat about in their gear they may tear easily. Thus, cadets are usually stationed in the crosstrees and the tops before the evolution begins so they can lay out onto the yards as soon as the sail is in its gear.

In heavy winds, the yard shoes may bind on their tracks, even when the halyard is slack. Thus, it is important for the cadets aloft and mast captains to make sure that the yards are in their fixed lifts before they lay out. Similarly, if there is slack in the braces, the yards may swing violently. The mast captain must ensure that all slack is removed before allowing cadets to furl. The slack created in the braces as the yards settle into their lifts should be rounded in on the lee side. The lead of the upper topsail braces requires rounding in on both braces. Brace captains must ensure that the yards do not slam into the backstays as they come down. In such cases, slack will have to be taken from the weather side.

When furling in heavy weather, the strongest cadet should lay out to the windward yardarm to smother the leech of the sail. Until the leech is controlled, the wind will continually catch the sail and blow it from the hands of those attempting to furl it. Once the weather leech is controlled, the rest of the sail can be quickly smothered and furled, working from weather to leeward. It may be beneficial to bring the ship up slightly into the wind so that the sails begin to lift. This reduces the tendency of the sails to blow away from the cadets on the yard. On the other hand, the sails should not be brought aback, in case they blow back on the cadets on the yards and possibly knock them from the footropes.

Staysails and headsails are doused by starting with the highest sail and working downward. Usually only a single sail at a time is doused in heavy weather, to prevent slatting and possible tearing. With the staysails, it is particularly important that the sheet be kept under control and that the halyard be eased as rapidly as possible. The sheet should be held to oppose the downhaul until the head of the sail has been hauled down to the miter seam—then it must be eased to fully douse the sail. In furling the staysails, cadets should work from the top down if there are not enough of them available to furl the entire sail at once. Otherwise, the wind may catch the sail and cause it to blow out the lower gaskets.

Heaving To

In very heavy weather, a point is reached where the ship cannot make way without pounding into the seas or putting excessive strain on the rigging. If there is sea room in such cases, the ship can *scud* (run directly downwind and down sea under little or no sail). *Scudding,* however, requires close control to prevent the ship from turning broadside into the trough and *broaching*. When in the trough, the *top-hamper* of the ship and heavy seas may result in dangerous rolling, which at its worst may part rigging or even capsize the ship.

If scudding is not attempted, the ship must *heave to,* to make the ride as comfortable and safe as possible. The purpose of heaving to is to have as little way on the ship as possible so that she rides up and over the seas rather than plowing through them. The safest course for heaving to is with the wind and seas on the bow or on the quarter. A slightly smoother ride is provided with the seas on the quarter, although the rudder is more exposed to damage by the seas. Also, there is more of a tendency to *broach* when the seas are on the quarter.

Any number of combinations of sails may be used to heave to, or in some cases it may be safest to douse all sail and use the main engine to hold *Eagle*'s course. The lower topsails are normally the square sails used because they are most easily handled and they are low enough to not cause excessive heel. The topmast staysails or mizzen staysail are used for the fore-and-aft sails because they too are low and have less tendency to heel the ship.

In heaving to with the seas on the bow, the fore topmast staysail, sheeted flat, can be used in combination with the main lower topsail, braced sharp, and the rudder lashed up. This arrangement causes the ship to slowly turn up into the wind until the lower topsail lifts, at which time the ship will lose way and the staysail will force the bow down to leeward until the topsail fills again. During this time the ship may roll heavily but usually not dangerously.

When heaving to with the wind on the quarter, the fore lower topsail should be used to keep the bow well off the wind and a mizzen staysail used to balance the ship and dampen the rolling. In this case, much closer rudder control is needed to prevent broaching or allowing the seas to come dead astern, possibly *pooping* the ship.

Eagle may roll heavily, regardless of how she heaves to. At times, waves will break on deck. Thus, the *heavy weather bill* must be set: lifelines are rigged on deck, all loose gear is lashed down, and the maximum watertight integrity is maintained. Fortunately, the weather is rarely so severe as to require heaving to. When rough weather necessitates action, however, a well-handled ship will ride moderately well when hove to.

Sailing in or near a Squall

Squalls are associated with the passage of weather fronts and with thunderstorms. In a squall there may be a sudden increase in wind speed—possibly up to hurricane force. Often this increase in speed is accompanied by a sudden wind shift of up to 180 degrees within a few minutes or even seconds. This combination of high winds and shifting direction can be extremely dangerous if the ship is under full sail and may catch her aback or *knock her down*.

Squalls can usually be detected both visually and on radar well before they strike. A prudent seaman will fall off and run before the squall. By running, the effective (relative) wind speed is reduced by the speed of the ship. Additionally, the ship will not heel as much, especially if upper square sails and staysails are set. With the seas and wind astern, sails can be taken in with comparative ease.

Many squalls do not contain high winds, however; if the ship ran off from every one sighted, she would be hard pressed to meet her schedule. Thus, on occasion *Eagle* will be caught before she can fall off or reduce sail. In such a situation, the ship will heel excessively. The increased submergence of the lee bow increases its lateral resistance and tends to force the bow up into the wind. Unless quick action is taken on the helm, the ship may get caught aback. In any case, an excessive amount of weather helm is needed to maintain course. Moreover, as the ship heels and the rudder becomes less vertical, its turning effect is lessened considerably. Thus, there is little residual helm available for falling off. Brailing in the spanker removes a tremendous force aft of the pivot point as well as some of the heeling moment and thus allows the bow to fall off and the rudder to be eased. An attempt to fall off may not be possible if the spanker is not brailed in.

In extremely strong winds, as the wind comes abeam, the heel may increase enough to knock her down. So, it may be necessary to ride the edge of the wind until the upper sails can be doused. Great care must be taken not to bring the wind too far forward in case the ship is caught aback, or too far aft in case she is knocked down. Normally, the extreme danger will have passed (even in a hurricane-force squall) once the royals, topgallants, and upper staysails have been taken in.

If the ship gets caught with the wind abeam and the heel increases dangerously, the sheets for the upper square sails and staysails may be thrown off. This action can tear the sails, but it may save the ship by spilling the wind in those sails that add most to the heel.

The decision to fall off or ride the edge of the wind must be made according to circumstances. Only forehandedness and experience ensure the right decision. Obviously, the best solution is to avoid the problem, if possible, by falling off or by reducing sail before the squall hits. When a squall approaches, it is prudent to fake out the spanker gear and be prepared to brail it in quickly if necessary.

GEAR FAILURE

Great care is taken in *Eagle* to prevent gear failure. Most of the running rigging is replaced annually; the standing rigging, all blocks, and all fittings are continually inspected and repaired when necessary. Nevertheless, gear failure may occur in heavy weather. The general procedure when gear carries away is to remove the strain from the affected area and to secure the gear from thrashing about so that repairs can be made.

Running Rigging Carried Away

If the *sheet* of a square sail carries away, the sail should be clewed up immediately to prevent it from ripping to shreds. It would be impossible to clew down the upper three yards since the clewline on the affected side would not have any effect in pulling the yard down. Nevertheless, clewing up causes most of the wind to be spilled from the sail. The yards usually come down by their own weight with the wind spilled.

If the *sheet* of a headsail or staysail carries away, the sail should be blanketed by falling off, and it should be doused as quickly as possible. In the case of a mizzen staysail, where the whipping sheet pendant and block may endanger personnel, the halyard should be thrown off even before the downhaul is manned. The force of the wind along the leech should douse the sail.

If the *downhaul* of a headsail or staysail parts, the ship should fall off. The force of the wind on the leech should be enough to force the sail down, or cadets may be stationed at the tack to pull it down by hand. If the sail jams, a line should be looped around the stay above the sail to pull the head down.

If a weather *brace* should carry away, the yard will fly up against the lee backstays, possibly imparting a dangerous strain on them. The ship should fall off so that some strain is taken by the other brace. The clewlines above and below the yard whose brace has carried away should be set taut to help control the yard. In marginal conditions where the ship is rolling, it may be beneficial to lash the yard against the backstays until a new brace can be rove.

If the *spanker sheet* carries away, the boom will slam violently against the mizzen backstays. The preventer should be hauled taut to control the boom and the sail brailed in as soon as possible. If the boom cannot be controlled by the preventer, it should be lashed to the backstays until a new sheet can be rove.

Standing Rigging and Gear Carried Away

If the *bobstay* or any *forward leading stay* parts, the vessel should be turned downwind to remove all strain. Sail should be reduced if the ship is laboring. A jury (makeshift) stay should be rigged. In the case of the bobstay, a chain can be passed from the end of the bowsprit through the hawsepipes and set taut with the capstan.

If a *backstay* or *shroud* parts, the OOD should wear ship immediately to place the strain on the opposite stay. Speed is of the essence here because the remaining stays will have to make up for the support of the damaged stay and a chain reaction might occur. After wearing, a new stay or preventer can be rigged.

If a *truss* or *shoe* carries away, the yard should be braced back and lashed in place. The sails bent and sheeted to it should be taken in before making repairs.

If a *yard* carries away, the lines attached to the spar, such as the sheets, clewlines, braces, and halyard should be handled in such a way as to minimize the motion of the yard to keep it from causing more damage. The spar should also be temporarily lashed in place to prevent it from causing more damage or crashing to the deck while gear is rigged to lower it. If a spar carries over the side, it should be recovered if possible. If it endangers the ship it should be cleared away immediately.

If there is a *steering casualty* caused by a failure in the linkage between the helm and the rudder, control should be shifted to after steering. The *trick wheel* is engaged by pulling the control handle forward to engage the gears. Sound-powered phone talkers should be assigned to relay commands from the bridge. After the casualty has been repaired, it will be necessary to set both the rudder and the *helm indicator* amidships and to line up the gears of the rudder mechanism with those of the main helm before pulling the control handle to engage the gears.

MAN OVERBOARD

The cry of "man overboard" strikes fear in the hearts of all sailors. For a square-rigger, not only is the possibility of someone going over the side more likely but only a well-trained and alert watch will react quickly enough to recover the lost shipmate. Even under power, *Eagle* is slower to respond and more difficult to maneuver than modern cutters. Under sail, the situation becomes even more difficult and the entire watch section must always be ready to respond. The officer of the deck is continually reevaluating wind and sea conditions throughout the watch and constantly rehearses the initial action that would be taken for the given conditions. The Ready Boat Crew must be properly organized and always ready to lower the boat away expeditiously.

Anyone seeing a crew member go over the side must sing out, "*Man overboard port (starboard) side*" and then ensure that the report reaches the bridge. As many life rings, marker buoys, and marker lights as possible are thrown to the person. A pipe is immediately made to inform all hands, and the station for stays alarm is sounded. *Eagle* will then be maneuvered to make the quickest and safest pickup possible. Under power, either a shipboard or a small boat pickup will be made. Under sail, the officer of the deck will order right or left full rudder to bring the ship up into the wind and *heave to*. Ships in company are notified by radio and by the use of the *Oscar* flag or man overboard lights (rapidly flashing not-under-command lights). If other vessels are nearby, the danger signal should be sounded to alert them and a broadcast made on channel 16. In the Combat Information Center (CIC), the ship's position should immediately be fixed by all means available. CIC will then report the estimated bearing and range to the person every thirty seconds using a dead reckoning plot. If the person is in sight, visual bearings should be taken on the bridge and passed back to CIC so that they can continually update their plot.

The height of eye on *Eagle*'s bridge is so low that the person may be quickly lost visually. The OOD must ensure that the person in the water is kept in sight by having cadets lay to the tops or shrouds to point to the person. Similarly, personnel on deck not otherwise engaged should point to the person to help the OOD maintain sight of the person in the water. When maneuvering to recover the person, it is very important that the OOD keep *Eagle* as close to the person as possible and make every effort to maintain visual contact.

Under Power

If under power, the engine may be used to bring the ship back to the vicinity of the person. The approach depends on wind and sea conditions and whether or not any sails are set. If a shipboard pickup is made, the vessel should be maneuvered to stop the ship slightly upwind of the person. Although there are a number of ways to maneuver in a man overboard situation, there are three basic options under power:

Back down. As already mentioned, *Eagle* does not respond as easily as most cutters. Therefore, it is sometimes best for the OOD to order "*Right/left full rudder*" to help swing the stern clear of the person and "*Engine back full*" at the same time. The stern will swing clear of the person and by the time the engine responds with astern turns, the person will be well clear of the screw. If the watch is alert and responds quickly, it will be possible to stop *Eagle* close enough to keep the person in sight. The small boat is immediately lowered and directed to make the pickup. This method is most effective when the ship is steaming at a standard bell or less but can be used at any time.

Modified destroyer turn. This type of pickup involves coming around a full 360 degrees, stopping upwind, and then drifting down on the person. With a single rudder and single screw, *Eagle* does not have a tight enough turning radius to complete a regular destroyer turn and return to the person in the water. Thus, it is important that the rudder be brought amidships for a brief period midway through the turn to ensure that a proper approach can be made. The OOD must be careful not to travel any farther from the person than necessary to be able to make the pickup. A boat may be lowered when the ship nears the person or a shipboard pickup can be made. In any case, a pipe should be made informing all hands as to the side and type of pickup.

Williamson turn. In low visibility or at night, the Williamson turn is generally preferred. The rudder is put over full in the direction of the person, but it is shifted once the ship's head has swung 60 degrees. This type of turn is also used when the OOD is unsure when the person was lost. *Eagle* should return to a reciprocal of her own track, and lookouts are stationed to look and listen for the missing person. A Williamson turn has the disadvantage of taking longer than a modified destroyer turn and it also carries the ship much farther away.

Under Sail Alone

If under sail alone, the ship should be brought up into the wind to stop all way, except when the weather is so severe that the ship may itself be endangered. After giving the helm command (left/right full rudder) to bring the ship up into the wind, the OOD should concentrate on lowering the boat and keeping the person in sight. The sails will take care of themselves until the full crew arrives on deck, at which time another officer can help with the sail handling commands.

When sufficient personnel have arrived on deck to handle sail, the command "*Let go and haul*" should be given to box the fore and main yards. In all man overboard situations under sail, when the ship is brought up into the wind, the command "Let go and haul" will be given, and the leeward small boat will be lowered as soon as possible.

The command "*Mainsail haul*" is not given because it is more important that the small boat be lowered as soon as possible. Although the command "Mainsail haul" will also stop the vessel and bring her to, it is an almost impossible command to execute while lowering the small boat since the mainsail sheets, main braces, and timenoguy are all inaccessible.

"Let go and haul," on the other hand, is a command that can be executed quickly using personnel from both the foremast and the mainmast while not interfering with the critical boat-lowering operation. It is most important that the yards be boxed and *Eagle* stop her headway, so that she will remain as close as possible to the person in the water and so the small boat may be lowered away as soon as possible.

After the foreyards have been braced, sails can be doused or trimmed as necessary. In coming up into the wind, the OOD should attempt to keep the bow from coming through the wind. As long as the vessel does not come head to wind a lee will be provided for the small boat. The ship will eventually lie to with the fore backing and the main drawing and drifting slowly downwind. The OOD should never turn downwind unless the ship would be endangered by being caught aback. Turning downwind will quickly carry *Eagle* away from the person in the water, and the ship could not be stopped without dousing all sail.

Whenever under sail, sail handling is done by personnel arriving on deck. The watch is completely engaged in lowering the boat away and the actual recovery of the person. As soon as the pipe "man overboard" is made, the engine room should immediately bring the main engine on the line and be prepared to answer bells as soon as possible. In an emergency, the main engine may be the most effective means of maneuvering the ship and lowering the small boat, even under sail.

Motor-Sailing

If motor-sailing, a careful judgment of circumstances must be made. In light winds or with only fore-and-aft sails set, it may be possible to make a shipboard pickup by using the engine to force the bow through the wind. In moderate winds it will probably be necessary to handle sails much as if the ship were under sail alone. They should normally be handled as in tacking, using the engine to make sure the bow passes through the wind. The actual method used when motor-sailing depends on the wind and sea conditions, and the sails set when the person goes overboard. Backing down and lowering a boat may be an option even with sails set.

COLLISION AVOIDANCE

So few square-rigged vessels remain afloat that meeting one at sea is something of a rarity and many power-driven vessels sighting one will come in for a closer look. This is not necessarily dangerous but since *Eagle* is not easily maneuvered under sail or power, the OOD must always be prepared to take action to avoid a close-quarters situation. As with any cutter, a sharp lookout must be maintained at all times. A record of visual bearings and a careful radar plot are maintained for all contacts to determine if risk of collision exists.

If risk of collision does exist, communications should be attempted on VHF-FM channel 16 (and/or channel 13 in U.S. coastal waters). When calling, the OOD should ensure that the other vessel understands that *Eagle* is a sailing vessel. Identifying yourself as the "Coast Guard sailing barque *Eagle*" or "United States Coast Guard tall ship *Eagle*" generally works well. If communications cannot be established to make a safe passing arrangement, the OOD may need to take action.

Under Power

Collision avoidance while under power is similar to that for any cutter. With low power and a single screw, however, action should be taken earlier, and changes in course and speed must be obvious to the other vessel. When under both sail and power, the OOD should remember that *Eagle* is considered a power-driven vessel and should display the appropriate navigational lights or day shape.

Under Sail Alone

When under sail alone, power-driven vessels must stay clear of *Eagle*. Unfortunately, not all vessels will recognize *Eagle* as a sailing vessel, particularly at night. First, it is more difficult to see a sailing vessel since she displays no white lights forward, and the red and green lights cannot be seen as far. Second, it is more difficult to determine *Eagle*'s aspect since there are no masthead lights, and side lights are the only indication another vessel will have as to her target angle. Also, in good winds, the heel of the ship may obscure the visibility of the leeward side light. Therefore, the OOD must do everything possible to make *Eagle* identifiable. At night, the sails may be illuminated with the sail flood lights, although care should be taken not to confuse the other vessel.

Since the maneuvering options open to the OOD are quite limited compared to those of a power-driven vessel, early action is particularly important to avoid a close-quarters situation. Increasing or decreasing speed by setting or taking in sail takes valuable time and thus is generally not an option as it would be on a power-driven vessel. Therefore, most often, the OOD will want to turn into the wind or fall off to avoid the other vessel. The OOD should always remember that it is more difficult to detect *Eagle*'s changes in aspect since there are no masthead lights. Therefore, when maneuvering, action not only must be early but also must be substantial.

Sail balance should also be considered before deciding to turn. When falling off, the spanker may have to be brailed in. One option always available is to order a full rudder turn into the wind and stop the ship by intentionally being caught aback. When under sail, this is the only way to stop the ship. This should be done only when there is no other safe way to avoid the other vessel, however, since it means having to call all hands on deck and also virtually eliminates any further maneuvering to avoid the other vessel.

Having the engine on the line is one of the safest ways to avoid endangering the ship and it should be used if necessary. Although not normally done, it may be put on line in five minutes or less in emergency situations. Therefore, an early decision must be made as to whether or not to order it up.

Minimizing Collision Damage

No one likes to think of collision, but forehanded evaluation of the possibilities can minimize the damage. Obviously, if at all possible, collision should be avoided. If action to avoid a collision has been unsuccessful or if the OOD is uncertain as to the intentions of the other vessel, the danger signal should be sounded. If a collision becomes imminent, the collision alarm must be sounded and the highest state of material readiness (Zebra) set. How the ship is maneuvered depends on wind and sea conditions and on the relative size and maneuverability of the two vessels.

The large size of *Eagle*'s compartments, the limited number of watertight bulkheads, and the location of the largest berthing areas amidships make it particularly important that *Eagle* not be hit broadside. In general, *Eagle* should be turned to reduce the relative speed between the two ships as much as possible so that a sideswipe, rather than a head-on collision, occurs. As a last resort it may be preferable to turn into the oncoming vessel and attempt a bows on approach. The bowsprit will absorb much of the force of a collision and, hopefully, will limit most of the damage to areas above the waterline. In all cases, decisions while in extremis should be made to avoid being hit broadside.

DECK SEAMANSHIP ▪ 8

BOAT LAUNCHING AND RECOVERY

Equipment

With some exceptions, the boat davits and associated boat-lowering equipment of *Eagle* are representative of the boat-handling gear of many ships. Most of the procedures and commands used on board *Eagle* are similar to those used by many modern cutters. The following gear is used in boat operations.

Boat davits are the quadrantal type. They are capable of carrying the boats rigged in or rigged out for sea. At sea, both boats are generally at the rail and ready to lower in case of a man overboard. This also allows more deck space for handling sail.

Boat falls of 4-inch, three-strand, right-laid manila line are rove through a two-fold purchase. The falls are belayed to a fitting on the davits called the *crucifix*. When not in use, the falls are stowed on reels. Before lowering, the falls are faked out athwartships on deck so that they are free for running.

The lower block of the falls is a nontoppling, double-sheaved block. An oval-shaped eye on the bottom of the lower block engages a spring-loaded safety hook on the *Rottimer releasing gear* in the boat. The Rottimer releasing gear is used to attach the boat to the falls. The spring-loaded hook in the boat, which attaches to the block, is normally held in the upright position by a slotted collar that may be rotated 180 degrees with a handle. The handle is held in the closed position with a lanyard. When the boat is lowered and the command "*Unhook*" is given, the lanyard is removed from the lever, the lever is swung 180 degrees to the open position, and the hook topples, releasing the eye of the block.

As soon as the falls are unhooked, the block is passed over the gunwale of the boat and the handle is rotated to the closed position and secured by a lanyard.

When hooking on, the eye of the block is swung smoothly past the spring-loaded keepers of the safety latch. The block must be held in an upright position while the slack is taken out of the falls. The bow and stern hook cadets must continue to hold on to the handles on the cheeks of the blocks, keeping them upright until the boat is clear of the water. The bow and stern hook cadets must be prepared to rotate the blocks to take any turns out of the falls.

A *frapping line* is tended on deck and controls the falls as the boat is raised and lowered. The falls are rove through a ring called a traveling lizard, at the end of the frapping line. The frapping lines keep the falls under control if the ship rolls.

The *sea painter* is used to tow the boat alongside the ship and provide a more stable platform for the boat crew. One end of the sea painter is secured to a cleat near the bow of the boat with a fid, the other end to a cleat in the waist of the ship. When the sea painter has been rigged properly, the coxswain can ride it under the boat falls and hook on without using the engine of the boat. The ship will generally maintain a slow ahead bell while the small boat is riding the sea painter.

Deck Detail

The lowering and recovery detail consists of the following personnel:

The *boatswain's mate of the watch* (BMOW) is in charge of lowering and recovering the boat. The BMOW is responsible for the overall supervision and safety of the operation. He or she must use standard commands and must give them in a loud clear voice so that everyone can hear.

Falls tenders. There are two cadets on each set of falls. One actually controls the falls and the other is a backup. When lowering the boat, the falls tenders keep their eyes on the crucifix, glance at the falls, and listen to the BMOW. The falls are smoothly eased *hand over hand,* but hands *must* be kept a forearm's distance *away from* the crucifix. When raising, the tenders watch the falls on the drum of the winch and listen to the BMOW.

Frapping line tenders. There is one cadet on each frapping line. Their job is to eliminate as much athwartship swing of the falls and boat as possible.

Sea painter tenders. One cadet retrieves the sea painter and coils it in preparation for passing when the boat returns and another cadet assists and is ready with a standby heaving line. There should be at least two heaving lines readily available.

Winch operator. The individual who operates the winch as directed by the BMOW.

Stoppers. Two cadets pass the stoppers on the falls when ordered.

Boat Crew

The *coxswain* is in charge of preparing the boat for launching and is also in charge of the boat as soon as it is waterborne. The coxswain ensures that the boat crew is in proper uniform and wearing life jackets or exposure suits, as appropriate. The coxswain also ensures that the boat crew are thoroughly familiar with their duties and are briefed before laying into the boat. The coxswain checks with the boat engineer as to the status of the engine, water, lube oil, and fuel. Except when unavoidable, a boat should never depart with less than a full tank of fuel. Finally, the coxswain should ensure that the boat is equipped with a VHF-FM radio and that a satisfactory communications check is made before lowering.

The *boat engineer* is responsible to the coxswain for the proper operation of the boat engine and for quickly making the necessary checks prior to and after lowering.

On the coxswain's order, the engineer starts the engine. When the boat is waterborne, the engineer ensures that the engine has seawater suction. The sea painter should not be cast off until the engine has seawater suction. While the boat is under way, the engineer makes checks of the engine to assure its continued proper operation. Note: Each boat receives a thorough daily checkout. They require only minimal checks before launching and in an emergency should always be ready to lower away.

The *bow hook* on command unhooks and hooks forward and tends the sea painter.

The *stern hook* on command unhooks and hooks aft.

Lowering the Boat

The procedure and commands for lowering the boat (assuming the boat is already rigged out) are:

BMOW: (After ensuring that all is ready on deck and that stations are properly manned.)

One cadet is told to "*Lay into the boat*" to remove lashings and make whatever checks are necessary. Anyone laying into the boat should be wearing a life jacket before getting into the boat.

BMOW: "*Cast off the gripe.*" This is done by one of the frapping line tenders.

BMOW: "*Cast off the preventers*" (if rigged). The cadet in the boat trips the pelican hooks on the preventers.

BMOW: "*Boat crew lay into the boat.*" The crew lays into the boat and grasps the manropes. As the boat is lowered and raised, each person should support most of his or her own weight on a manrope in case the boat should fall.

Coxswain: When satisfied that all is ready in the boat, informs the BMOW, "*Ready in the boat.*"

BMOW: Reports to the OOD, "*Ready on deck.*"

BMOW: Receives permission from the OOD and commands, "*On the falls. Take off all but one round turn and half of a figure eight.*"

BMOW: Inquires, "*Ready forward/aft?*"

BMOW: Upon confirmation that both falls are ready, commands, "*Lower away together,*" then "*Lively* or *Easy forward/aft*" as appropriate. This keeps the boat on an even keel.

BMOW: As the ship rolls toward the boat, and the boat is lifted onto a swell, commands, "*Let fall.*" At this point the coxswain is in charge.

Coxswain: Commands, "*Unhook aft.*" After receiving the report and visually confirming that the after falls are unhooked, commands, "*Unhook forward.*" Note: The after falls are always unhooked before the forward falls when lowering.

Coxswain: When the falls are clear, the coxswain sheers the boat out riding on the sea painter, and when permission is received from the bridge, commands, "*Cast off the sea painter.*" (Do not cast off the sea painter until the engine has seawater suction and a catenary is in the sea painter.)

Recovering the Boat

The procedures and commands for raising the boat are:

BMOW to OOD: "*Ready on deck,*" when rigged to pick up the boat and all personnel are at their assigned stations.

Coxswain: "Permission to come alongside and receive the sea painter."

OOD: "*Come alongside and receive the sea painter.*"

Coxswain: When the boat is paralleling the course and speed of the ship and is ready to receive the sea painter, commands, "*Pass the sea painter.*" The cadet on deck passes a heaving line to which the sea painter is attached. The bow hook makes the sea painter fast to the bow cleat of the boat using a fid, and the coxswain then rides the sea painter.

OOD: "*Lay under the falls and hook on.*"

Coxswain: When under the davits with the falls in position commands, "*Hook on forward.*" When hooked on forward, commands, "*Hook on aft.*" When raising the boat, the forward falls are always hooked first.

Coxswain: When all is ready in the boat, reports, "*Ready in the boat.*"

Note: At this point the BMOW is again in charge.

BMOW: "*Heave around together.*" The cadet on the winch moves the control lever to slow, then immediately to high speed.

The commands "*Lively*" and "*Easy*" are not used when raising with a winch. To level the boat, it may be necessary to go slower on one fall, and the command "*Surge forward/aft*" is given by the BMOW. To comply, the falls tender allows the turns on the appropriate drum of the winch to slip. When the boat is on an even keel, the command "*Heave around together*" is again given.

BMOW: When the boat is at the rail, commands, "*Avast heaving.*" The cadet on the winch moves the control to stop and the falls are held on the drum.

BMOW: "*Boat crew lay out of the boat.*"

BMOW: When the crew is out of the boat, commands, "*Pass your stoppers fore and aft.*"

BMOW: When informed "*Stoppers passed fore/aft,*" commands, "*On the forward falls, back easy.*" The strain is then transferred from the winch drum to the passed stopper. If the stopper holds, it is reported to the BMOW by the cadet passing the stopper ("Stopper holding forward"). The BMOW commands, "*On the forward falls, up behind.*" The forward falls are belayed to the crucifix.

If the stopper does not hold, the BMOW will command, "*Set taut,*" and the strain will again be taken by the winch until the stopper is passed again. When the falls are secured forward, the BMOW commands, "*On the after falls, back easy,*" and the process is repeated for the after falls. After the falls have been belayed, the boat davits are cranked in, the gripe is passed and made up securely, all gear is stowed, and lines are made up.

Safety Notes

Each member of the boat crew, and anyone going into the boat for any reason, must wear a life jacket as well as ask permission from the OOD. Manropes are provided for the safety of the boat crew. They must be used whenever the boat is not completely rigged for sea.

The most critical phase of the raising and lowering operations is the transition between the time the boat is fully waterborne and the time that it is clear of the water. During this time, the boat and falls are under the greatest stress because of the working of the ship in the seaway. This period must be minimized by rapid raising or lowering.

All personnel involved should remain alert, pay attention to their immediate job, and keep silent unless required to speak. The OOD should always ensure that the ship provides a good lee for the boat, and that the ship is as stable as possible when lowering or raising.

ANCHORING

Ground Tackle

Eagle has two anchors. The port anchor has ten shots of chain and the starboard anchor eleven shots. Anchor chains are marked according to the normal Coast Guard system with fifteen fathoms per shot. The first shot includes the bending and swivel shots.

Ground Tackle Operation

The anchor-handling gear consists of two separate electrically driven capstans coupled through a clutch to the wildcats (drums with sprockets that hold the links of the anchor chain as it is raised or lowered). The gears and shafting between the capstans are below the fo'c'sle deck. Aft of each wildcat is a two-position lever that engages it to the capstan. On top of each wildcat is a handwheel clutch control. It is used to disengage the wildcat so that it will run freely when the anchor is let go and to engage it when the chain is to be heaved around. When the anchor is let go, the chain is controlled by a band-type brake controlled by a handwheel aft of each wildcat.

Before 1954, the anchor was weighed by hand in the traditional manner by turning a capstan with capstan bars placed in pigeon holes. This gear remained on board until the late 1970s. A similar capstan remains on board on the fantail and is used to handle the aft mooring lines.

Chain stoppers consisting of several chain links, a turnbuckle, and a *pelican hook* are provided for each chain. These chain stoppers are shackled to padeyes on the deck and secured to the anchor chain forward of the wildcat. The pelican hook is used to secure the anchor for sea, to hold it when it is made ready for letting go, and to hold the anchor in the hawsepipe in case the need arises to unshackle the chain from the anchor. Immediately forward of the chain stoppers are two cat's pawls. These are safety devices that would hold the anchor should a chain stopper or the brake fail.

When word is passed to prepare to bring the ship to anchor, the first lieutenant, who is normally in charge on the fo'c'sle, musters the anchor detail. The OOD will pass whether the port or starboard anchor is to be used. If not done earlier, the anchor detail requests that the engine room provide power to the anchor windlasses. The OOD should have already notified the engine room that the ship will be anchoring. Both anchors are made ready for letting go. In addition, the anchor detail receives any special instructions and is advised as to the depth of the water and type of bottom.

It is very rare that a person has a reason to be in the chain locker. It is mandatory, however, that the anchor detail ascertain that no person is in the chain locker. It is also wise to inspect the chain in the bin to ensure that it isn't fouled.

If an anchor buoy is used, the buoy should have sufficient scope on the buoy line to ensure that it will reach the surface. The line should be short enough, however, to ensure that it will float almost directly over the anchor.

The wildcat is engaged for the anchor, which is being prepared for letting go. A light strain is taken on the chain. At the same time, the brake is backed off. An additional strain is taken on the chain, if necessary, until it is possible to raise the cat's pawl. The brake is then set and the windlass stopped. The pelican hook of the chain stopper is moved back two links and reattached. The direction of the windlass is reversed, the brake eased, and the chain walked out (eased out slowly, link by link) until the strain is taken by the *pelican hook* and there is slack between the chain stopper and the wildcat.

The windlass is stopped, the brake is again set taut, and the clutch of the wildcat is disengaged. The two links of chain have been backed out so that it is known that the anchor is not jammed in the hawsepipe and so that the entire strain of the anchor is taken by the *pelican hook/chain stopper*. With the strain on the stopper, the anchor can be let go by tripping the pelican hook. No other controls need be adjusted.

It may be that the anchor has been ordered walked out to the water's edge or, when anchoring in deep water, even further. The same process is used except that the distance is greater than two links.

Letting Go

When the ship nears the desired anchorage, the word is passed from the bridge to "*Stand by to let go the starboard (port) anchor.*" The first lieutenant orders the brake released, orders all hands abaft the wildcats, and orders the pin removed from the retaining bail on the pelican hook. At this point, the anchor detail is normally advised as to the desired scope of chain and whether it will be measured "*on deck*" or "*at the water's edge.*" This scope is an integral number of shots and is expressed as "*One shot on deck*" or "*Three shots at the water's edge.*"

When the ship comes to the desired position,

the command is given from the bridge to "*Let go of the starboard (port) anchor*." This command must be executed without delay. The retaining bail on the pelican hook is knocked free with a maul and the anchor is let go. The crew member whose duty it is to tend the brake allows the anchor to run freely until it touches the bottom, at which time a few turns are set upon the brake to prevent the chain from overhauling itself and piling up on the bottom.

Since the chain runs rapidly and often throws off rust chips, everyone in the immediate area must wear a protective face mask or goggles. The ship should have slight sternway at this point. The chain is allowed to *veer* to the desired scope, at which time the brake is set. If the ship were not moving, the anchor chain would pile up on the bottom and might foul the anchor. During this time, the person in charge makes reports to the bridge as to how the chain is tending, using the "clock" system (12 o'clock being dead ahead), and the amount of strain on the chain.

When the anchor has taken a good bite in the bottom the anchor detail reports, "*Anchor brought to and holding*." Unless it is desirable to veer chain, the anchor detail will make the anchor ready for heaving around. The chain stopper is passed. The brake is backed off so that the strain will be on the pelican hook, and the chain between the wildcat and the pelican hook becomes slack. The wildcat will be engaged. The brake is then set taut and the cat's pawl is dropped. No strain comes on the pawl, for it is merely a safety device to be used if the pelican hook fails. If some of the strain is allowed to be taken by the pawl, it might not be possible to veer chain if necessary until the chain is heaved in to release the strain on the pawl.

Weighing Anchor

Before weighing anchor, the engine room is notified so that sufficient electrical power is available to operate the windlass and enough fire main pressure is available to wash down the chain and anchor as they are heaved in. When the anchor detail is set the following are checked:

1. Sufficient personnel are available.
2. The wildcat clutch is engaged.
3. One or more fire hoses are rigged to wash down the anchor and chain as they come on board.
4. No person or foreign object is in the chain locker.

The anchor detail then reports, "*Anchor detail manned and ready to heave around.*" When the order to heave around is given, the windlass is engaged and the brake is backed off a few turns. When the pelican hook goes slack, it is knocked clear and the brake backed off all the way. The pawl remains down and rides over each link as it comes on board. This is a safety feature used in case something should happen to the wildcat. As the chain is being heaved in, reports are made to the bridge about the direction the anchor is tending and the amount of strain on the chain.

When the anchor comes to short stay (when all slack chain has been heaved in and the anchor is just about to be lifted from the bottom), the anchor detail *avasts* heaving and reports, "*Anchor at short stay.*" Should there be a delay in any of the other preparations for getting under way, the vessel will still be somewhat anchored. With the captain's permission, the OOD will order the anchor detail to "*Break out the anchor.*" Heaving around is resumed. As soon as the anchor breaks out, the anchor windlass speeds up and the report "*Anchor's aweigh*" is made.

Next comes the order "*House the anchor.*" The anchor is heaved into the hawsepipe, the brake set taut, and the windlass stopped. Great care must be exercised here, as a severe strain can come on the anchor windlass. If allowed to continue too far, great damage may be done. When the brake has been set taut, the chain stopper is passed. Unless orders to the contrary are received, the anchor is again made ready for letting go and remains ready until the special sea detail and the anchor detail are secured. The anchors are then made ready for sea and the engine room advised that the windlass is secured.

RIGGING GEAR ALOFT

Bending on a Square Sail

First, the sail is stretched along the deck, after side down, and the head is stretched taut. The sail is then gathered up as in furling and gaskets are passed snugly around it, leaving the tabling at the head and foot clear. For sails with leechlines or bunt-leechlines, the leech cringles are also exposed.

A *gantline* is then passed around the center of the sail and it is swayed aloft to the yard where it is to be bent. The sail is hoisted far enough above the yard so that cadets can grasp it by the head cringles and haul it out along the yard as the gantline is eased. As soon as possible, the head earing is taken through its eye on the yardarm and brought back through the head cringle. This then serves as a tackle to help extend the head of the sail.

The sail is hauled out with the head earings and the gantline is further slacked until the special hooks on the earing jackstays on the yardarms can be passed through the head cringles. The sail is then carefully centered on the yard and the center roband is passed and secured. An additional turn is taken with the head earing, or in the case of the lower sails, a jigger is hooked into the head cringles. The tabling along the head of the sail is stretched taut, after which the head earings are secured and remaining robands are passed around the jackstays. Sheets, clewlines, leechlines, bunt-leechlines, and buntlines are bent to the sail; it is then ready for setting. In bending the gear, considerable care and foresight are necessary to avoid fouling and to ensure that everything will run fair when the sail is set. As soon as possible, the sail should be set to ensure that everything is properly rigged.

Bending on a Fore-and-Aft Sail

A fore-and-aft sail is made up along the foot and swayed up to the stay upon which it is bent. The halyard is bent into the head cringle, and the tack is made fast. The luff of the sail is then bent to the hanks on the stay, starting at the head and then working down. In a harbor or in fair weather, this may be accomplished most easily by running the sail partly up the stay as the robands are passed on the individual hanks. The sheets and downhaul are shackled to the clew cringle and the sail is ready to set.

RAISING AND LOWERING THE TOPGALLANT MASTS

Eagle was designed to be able to transit the Kiel Canal in Germany, where the vertical clearance is approximately 135 feet. Since the height of the fore and main masts is 147.3 feet, (originally 150.3 feet), the topgallant masts were designed to be lowered by about 15 feet. *Eagle* today must house the topgallant masts to transit up the Thames River to her homeport at the U.S. Coast Guard Academy, New London, Connecticut. The process first requires the topgallant yard to be unshipped and secured in a special *winter housing*, a fitting on the forward part of the topmast cap band. The topgallant mast is then lowered by means of the upper topsail halyard purchase, which has been rigged to a mast rope.

The procedure for housing and stepping the mast is complicated and requires trained personnel. It can be very dangerous and is normally only done by the enlisted deck force. As a result, the procedures are designed for persons already expert in seamanship rather than for cadets. Detailed procedures are outlined in current *Eagle* directives. With a trained crew and good weather, both masts can be housed or stepped in under five hours. This procedure is normally done at anchor or while moored to ensure that full attention can be devoted to the stepping or housing operation. Providing a stable platform is important and the weather decks should be cleared of all unnecessary personnel.

FULL-DRESSING SHIP

Coast Guard ships are dressed or full-dressed on national holidays and for special ceremonies. The procedures for dressing and full-dressing are prescribed by *U.S. Coast Guard Regulations* and the U.S. Navy publication *Flags and Pennants.*

When full-dressing ship, a rainbow of signal flags, arranged in the order prescribed in *Flags and Pennants,* is displayed. It reaches from the foot of the jackstaff to the mastheads and then to the foot of the flagstaff. For *Eagle,* the procedure for rigging the rainbow is as follows:

1. Jackstaff to foremast: A block is set above the fore royal stay on the forward side of the mast; the halyard is secured at the foot of the jackstaff and rove through the block down to the fore crosstrees; the halyard is marked 150 feet from the base of the jackstaff; and the first twenty-five flags are bent on in accordance with the order listed in *Flags and Pennants.* The hooks are connected to the snap rings of the flags and are made free for running at the foot of the jackstaff.

2. Foremast to mainmast: The distance from the fore truck to the main truck is 88 feet and requires the next thirteen flags in order. Blocks are placed on the after side of fore truck and the forward side of main truck. The halyard is rove from the fore crosstrees through the fore truck block and down to the main crosstrees; the thirteen flags are bent on and made up for running. The foremast to mainmast flags are set from the

Fig. 44. Full-dress ship stations

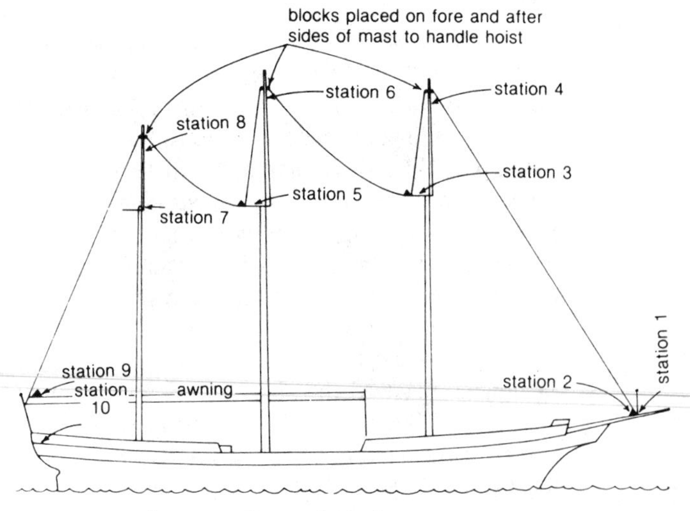

▲	Denotes flags piled and ready for running.
station 1:	Two cadets to handle flag on staff.
station 2:	Two cadets to handle fore triangle flags.
station 3:	Two cadets to tend halyards; one cadet to handle fore-to-main flags.
station 4:	One cadet to place blocks and observe hoist; handles fouls and other emergencies at blocks.
station 5:	Two cadets to tend halyards; one cadet to handle main-to-mizzen flags.
station 6:	One cadet to place blocks and observe hoist; handles fouls and other emergencies at blocks.
station 7:	Three cadets to tend halyards and handle flags as required.
station 8:	One cadet to place blocks and observe hoist; handles fouls and other emergencies at blocks.
station 9:	One cadet to tend mizzen-to-flagstaff flags.
station 10:	Two cadets to handle flag on staff.

main crosstrees and are set taut from the fore crosstrees.

3. Mainmast to mizzenmast: The distance from the main truck to the mizzen truck is 68 feet and requires the next twelve flags in order. Blocks are set, similar to those from the foremast to the mainmast; likewise, halyards are rove and twelve flags are bent on free for running with this halyard and the flags stopped off on the main crosstrees. The mainmast to mizzenmast flags are set from the mizzen top and are set taut from the main crosstrees.

4. Mizzenmast to flagstaff: The distance from the mizzenmast to the flagstaff, at the level of awning, is 107 feet and requires the next nineteen flags in succession. The halyard is secured on the flagstaff at the point level with the awning and is rove through a block, previously rigged on the after side of the mizzen truck, down to the mizzen top. The halyard is marked 107 feet from the flagstaff, and the nineteen flags previously designated are bent on and faked out free for running on top of the awning.

RIGGING GEAR ON DECK

Cargo Boom

The cargo boom was formerly used for launching and recovering small boats that were located in chocks on the *gallows frame* above the laundry. Since these boats have been removed, the boom is now used only when loading or unloading heavy gear (fig. 45). There are four lines that must be rigged to handle the boom: the topping lift, two vangs, and the whip.

Fig. 45. Cargo boom rigging

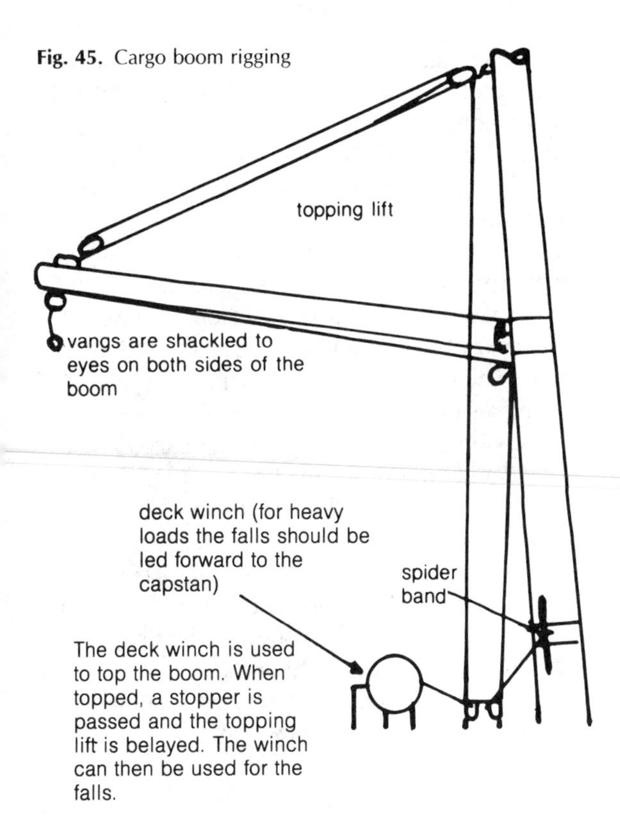

1. The *topping lift* is used to adjust the height of the boom. The lift consists of a three-fold purchase that runs from an eye just below the main top to one at the head of the boom. When the boom is not being used, the topping lift is usually left shackled to the fitting on the mast; the block that attaches to the head of the boom is seized off out of the way at the base of the mast or at the spider band. Thus, the first step in rigging the

boom is to shackle the lower topping lift block to the head of the boom. The hauling end of the lift is led through a fairlead block at the base of the mast and then to the waist deck winch. When the boom is topped, the lift is secured to the cleat just below the spider band on the mast.

2. The *vangs* are used to control the athwartships motion of the boom. Unless an unusually heavy load is to be handled, tackles are shackled into the eyes on each side of the head of the boom. The lower end of the tackles are shackled to padeyes on deck. The choice of padeyes to use depends on the side on which the cargo is to be worked and on how far the boom must be swung. In general, the vangs should lead as close to right angles from the boom as possible.

3. The *whip* or *hoist* is a purchase permanently rigged between the head and foot of the boom. When the boom is to be used, the hauling end of the purchase is run through a fairlead at the base of the mast to the winch. The whip should be led to the opposite winch drum from the topping lift so that both lines can be worked together.

Handling the boom is simple but requires great care to ensure a safe operation. The boom is first topped by hauling on the topping lift purchase and easing the vangs. When topped, a stopper is passed and the purchase is belayed on the spider band. The boom is then centered over the load by means of the vangs, hauling on one and easing the other. The *whip* is attached to the load and hauled up by the winch.

The load should be lifted only to the height necessary to clear obstructions. When swinging the boom with a load, personnel handling the vangs must be extremely careful to keep the load under control. Thus, close coordination is needed between the people working each vang. All loads should be rigged with tag (steadying) lines to keep the load under control.

Rigging the Accommodation Ladder

The accommodation ladder consists essentially of an upper and lower platform connected by a ladder. The lower end of the ladder, which is connected to the lower platform, is held in place by a bridle which is supported by the fish davit. The lower platform is equipped with fenders to protect boats from being damaged when coming alongside. The procedure for rigging the accommodation ladder is not difficult. Due to the weight and cumbersome size, however, it is imperative that the initial rigging be done properly. Rigging the accommodation ladder can take several hours and is generally done by the enlisted deck force. The main yard is used as a boom to lift the ladder over the side and lower it into position. The OOD should ensure that a stable platform is provided while the rigging operation is in progress. Personnel working over the side should be wearing safety shoes, hard hats, and life jackets.

Rigging Boat Booms

Boat booms allow small boats to moor well clear of the sides of ships lying at anchor or moored to a mooring buoy. The order for a boat alongside to moor to a boom is "Haul out to the port (starboard) boom." A boat boom (fig. 46) consists of a stout spar secured by its gooseneck (inboard end

Fig. 46. Starboard boat boom rigged. Small boat hauled out to boom.

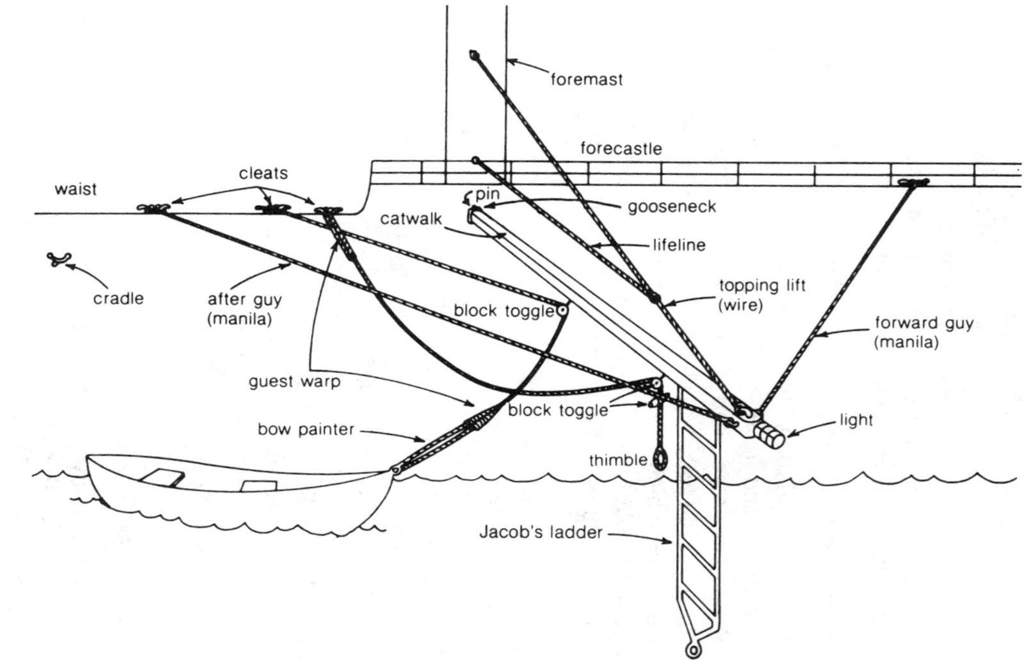

fitting) to a pin in the side of the ship. This allows free motion fore and aft in a horizontal plane. The outboard end of the boom hangs from a topping lift, which is a single wire with a chain length in the lower end. The topping lift keeps the boom constantly at the proper height. Fore-and-aft motion of the boom is controlled by lines called forward and after guys.

A strong two- or three-inch nylon line called a *guest warp* leads from a forward point on the ship out through a block at the outboard end of the boom. The outboard end of the guest warp is spliced around a metal thimble through which boats reeve their bow lines. A toggle is seized between strands of the guest warp, above the thimble to keep the latter from running up out of reach when a boat lets it go.

One or more *Jacob's ladders* hanging from the boom make it possible for boat crews to get on board *Eagle*. The lifeline is made from a two-inch line and is approximately three feet above the catwalk. One end is made fast to the topping lift; the other end is secured to the ship's railing or a stanchion.

Rigging out the boom is a simple process. The boom stows in a chock alongside, with its outboard end aft. The ladder, guys, topping lift, and guest warps are attached first. The guys lead out fore and aft with slack faked out free for running. A two-fold purchase is secured to a padeye on deck and to the topping lift. The boom is topped up to clear the chock. The boom is started out with a shove from a boat hook and the forward guy is hauled hard until the after one comes taut. This initial push is important since the boom has to travel three or four feet for the forward guy to be able to haul the boom out perpendicular to the hull. It takes five to ten cadets to haul the boom out with the forward guy.

A boat is always made fast to a guest warp by the bight of its bowline, with the end secured back in the boat. This allows for quick release. The boat always rides to a long lead on the bowline. The shorter the lead, the more vertical the strain, and the more of the boat's weight there is on the bowline as she rides up and down on swells. Boats at booms have parted their lines or pulled out cleats or padeyes because the leads on their bowlines were too short. Anyone traveling over a boat boom must wear a life jacket, use the lifeline, and exercise caution.

In securing the boat boom, the boom is topped with the topping lift until the boom makes about a 30-degree angle with the horizon. The forward guy is eased handsomely. The boom is always below the gunwale as it comes in and a fender is available to absorb the shock as the boom comes alongside. *Eagle* has a short single boat boom to port and a long double boat boom to starboard.

WATERTIGHT INTEGRITY

Buoyancy and stability are two essential attributes of any ship; they must be preserved if she is to continue to float and to sail. Numerous compartments with watertight boundaries and proper distribution of weight ensure that the vessel has both buoyancy and stability.

Flooding of water into a compartment that is designed to be dry will decrease buoyancy. It is likely to have an adverse effect upon stability by introducing weight in the wrong place. Therefore, a prime concern in ship construction is watertight integrity. Ideally, all watertight bulkheads would be continuous with no possible sources of leakage: no doors, hatches, port lights, vent ducts, or cable runs through bulkheads. There must be access to each space, however, and habitability demands cable runs and ventilation. So designers have to compromise between watertight integrity and operational usability. They break the watertight boundaries to provide the necessary access.

Still, the ship must be capable of being made watertight in the event of a collision or grounding. Water that might accidentally enter the hull must be prevented from flooding progressively from one compartment to the next. In order to maintain watertight integrity in boundaries containing openings, each fitting is provided with a watertight designation. If all fittings were closed, the ship should be watertight. There would be no access, however. Each such opening of a watertight fitting reduces the total watertight integrity somewhat. To have knowledge of the extent to which it has been diminished, there must be a record of what fittings are open. The watertight integrity maintained in U.S. Coast Guard and Navy vessels at a particular time is called its *material condition*.

Although this procedure maintains good control over watertight integrity, it can be more restrictive than is needed outside of wartime or very heavy weather. Under some circumstances, it is reasonable to allow frequently used access doors to be opened. Personnel are close enough to the fittings to close them promptly in case of accident.

There are three different standard material conditions that may be prescribed for *Eagle,* depending upon the degree of watertight integrity required.

These are:

1. Material Condition **Xray:** The most relaxed condition. Suitable for daytime while in port.
2. Material Condition **Yoke:** An intermediate condition used at night when in port and at all times under way.
3. Material Condition **Zebra:** The most secure material condition in which the ship can continue to operate. Suitable for extremely heavy weather, attack, or when damage is imminent.

To determine what fittings are to be open or closed in each of the material conditions, each fitting is classified according to its function and importance. A letter (*X, Y, Z,* or *W*) indicating the classification is attached to each fitting and the following closure table is applied:

Material Condition	**Classification**			
	X	Y	Z	W
Xray	Closed	Open	Open	Open
Yoke	Closed	Closed	Open	Open
Zebra	Closed	Closed	Closed	Open

A label with a circle around it is designated as *circle Xray (yoke, zebra).* This circle indicates that the fitting (usually hatches and watertight doors) may be opened for passage without obtaining permission from the officer of the deck as long as the fitting is immediately secured again.

Whenever it becomes necessary to open a fitting that is supposed to be closed according to the material condition in effect, permission must be obtained from the officer of the deck. When requesting permission, you must give the name and rank/rate of the person making the request, the type of fitting, the number of the fitting, the classification of the fitting, and the reason for the request. When permission is given to open a fitting, this information is logged with the time in the Damage Control Closure Log. The closure of a fitting is reported promptly and is also logged.

Glossary

Note: Terms enclosed by quotation marks are used as commands.

aback. A sail is aback when the wind strikes it on the forward side; this can be intentional in maneuvering or unexpected in a sudden wind shift.

abeam. A direction away from either side of a vessel (90 degrees or 270 degrees relative to the ship's heading).

after steering. The emergency steering station located on the fantail that is engaged if there is a casualty to the main steering station on the bridge.

amidships. The portion of a vessel midway between the bow and stern or midway between the port and starboard sides.

anemometer. An instrument used to measure the direction and speed of the wind. The sensor for the anemometer is located on the mizzenmast. The anemometer gives the relative wind direction and speed.

astern. A direction behind a vessel (180 degrees relative to the ship's heading).

"Avast." Immediately stop executing the last command and hold what you have. Do not belay until directed. Used only when continuing will endanger gear or personnel. The normal command would be, "That's well."

back. 1. In the Northern Hemisphere, a change in the wind direction in a counterclockwise direction. 2. Intentionally causing the sails to be aback, as in tacking.

"Back easy." Slowly ease the line, either to check a stopper or to take turns on or off a belaying pin.

backstay. Standing rigging leading from a point on the mast to the rail abaft the mast.

bagpipe. Backing the spanker by hauling it amidships and then to windward using the weather preventer, to create a greater turning moment. Sometimes used when tacking in light air.

barque. A sailing vessel with three or more masts whose after mast is fore-and-aft rigged. Note: *Eagle* is not a *ship*. She is called one only for convenience in this manual. A *ship* is square-rigged on all masts.

barquentine. A sailing vessel with three or more masts whose foremast is square-rigged and after masts are rigged fore and aft.

"Belay." Secure a line to a belaying pin, cleat, or other point established for this purpose.

bend. 1. To fasten a sail securely to the jackstay on a yard by means of robands. 2. A method of fastening one line to another.

binnacle. The wooden housing for the ship's magnetic steering compass.

blanket. A sail is blanketed when the wind is prevented from striking it, either by another vessel passing close aboard to weather or by the sails on another mast on the same ship.

"Board the tack." Secure a special tackle called the *tack-jigger* to the weather clew of the foresail or mainsail and haul it down to the rail. Used when sailing close-hauled.

bobstay. A heavy stay (a steel rod on *Eagle*) running from the stem of the ship to the end of the bowsprit. Provides support for the bowsprit.

boltrope. Roping around the edges of a sail. See also **tabling.**
boom. 1. A spar used to support the foot of the spanker. 2. A spar used to extend the reach of a line for handling cargo or in mooring boats, as in the cargo boom and boat boom.
bowsprit. The large spar on the bow of a sailing vessel. Provides a good lead for the stays that support the mast and the headsails.
boxhauling. Sailing maneuver for changing tacks that is used in confined waters when there is not sea room to tack and the loss of ground in wearing is unacceptable.
boxing. A maneuver that can be used when caught aback if the wind is still on the weather bow. The fore and main yards are braced on opposite tacks providing enough force to push the bow off the wind; also used in man overboard situations or to slow the ship when heaving to.
braced square. Yards braced so that they are perpendicular to the heading of the ship.
braces. Lines used to move the yards in a horizontal plane.
bracing. Swinging the yards in a horizontal plane.
brails. Lines used to haul the spanker in to the mast when dousing.
broach. To be thrown broadside to a heavy surf or sea.
bull's eye. Circular piece of hardwood hollowed in the center. Has a groove around it for a strop and a hole for the lead of a line. Used to change the lead of a line where a block is not required.
bumpkins. Steel supports extending outboard from the sides of a square-rigger to support

blocks for the braces and to lead them clear of the ship.
bunt-leechlines. Lines on the square sails used to furl the square sails by bringing the leech and foot up to the yard.
buntlines. Lines used to douse a square sail that haul the foot up to the yard.

cap. A band at the head of the mast. In older sailing vessels the cap held the lower part of the topmasts to the lower masts.
carry away. To fail or to break loose, as in lines parting, sails tearing, or spars coming unhoused as a result of excessive strain.
cast or casting. To swing the vessel's head as necessary when maneuvering under power (also called *back and fill*).
catenary. A dip in a line or chain caused by the weight of the line itself. The *catenary* provides a spring or elastic effect.
caught aback. The ship is caught aback when, because of a wind shift or helmsman error, the wind strikes the forward rather than the after side of the square sails.
chafing. The wearing down of ropes, lines, sails, or other parts of the ship by the rubbing action caused by the ship's motion or wind.
chapell. A recovery maneuver used when caught aback and the wind has shifted to the opposite bow; the main yards are braced square to the ship, the stern is backed into the wind, and the ship is wore around.
cheek blocks. Blocks attached to the yardarms through which square sail sheets are led.

"Clear away." Lay out a coil so that the line will run freely. Applies to downhauls, weather staysail sheets, and so on. Also used to refer to striking the tack-jigger.
clew. The lower corners of a square sail or the after lower corner of a fore-and-aft sail.
"Clew down." Haul on the clewlines while holding the sheets in order to settle a yard into its fixed lifts.
clew-garnet. Special term for the clewlines of the foresail and mainsail.
"Clew up." To haul a sail up into its gear by easing the sheets and hauling on the clewlines, buntlines, and leechlines.
close-hauled. Point of sail where a vessel is sailing as near to the wind as possible. (Also, *full and by* and *on the wind.*)
cockbill. Yards are cockbilled when they are canted with respect to the horizontal. When sails are furled, the upper yards will cockbill when braced sharp. When sails are set, cockbill is adjusted by the fore and main lifts. Cockbill can only be removed in the upper three yards when sails are set.
come-along. A chain or wire tackle with a ratchet mechanism used to lift or take a strain as the ratchet is engaged.
courses. Collective term for both the mainsail and foresail.
crane lines. Athwartships lines or wire rope for cadets to work between the shrouds—similar to ratlines.
cringle. Ring or grommet worked into the tabling of a sail at the head, clew, or leech. Used to make lines or rope fast.

crosstrees. Athwartships timbers located where the topmast and topgallant mast come together.

deadman. An improperly furled section of a sail that looks as if a "dead man" could be furled inside it.

dograil. (Sometimes called *knightshead.*) The first timbers on either side of the stem, forming the seat of the bowsprit. On board *Eagle*, the headsail downhauls are belayed to pins on the dograil.

dolphin striker. A strut or brace extending almost vertically downward from the bowsprit to the bobstay.

douse. To take in a sail.

downhaul. Line leading from the deck through the head of a staysail and down to the clew used for dousing.

earing. A short piece of line secured to a cringle used to make fast. For hauling out the upper corners of the head of a square sail when bending it to its yard.

"Ease." Pay out slowly and with care; reduce strain on the line.

fairlead. A block or fitting that changes the direction (lead) of a line without giving mechanical advantage, or that allows it to run free without chafing (fair).

fairlead board. A board with holes in it for running rigging to pass through.

fall off. When a sailing vessel changes course in a direction away from the wind.

falls. The line in a tackle that is rove through the blocks to create a mechanical advantage.

fanning. Bracing the weather yardarms slightly aft for each yard as you go higher. Used to take advantage of the differences in relative wind speeds at different altitudes off the water.
fid. A wooden marlinspike (pointed tool to separate strands of rope) used primarily to splice line but also used to secure a sea painter to a small boat.
fife rail. A rail around three sides of each mast, used to belay running rigging.
flemish horse. A footrope at the tip of a yard.
flukes. The broad flat sections of the anchor that actually dig into the bottom. The flukes can rotate on the anchor stock. Occasionally when the anchor is weighed, the flukes will point in toward the hull and will have to be tripped or rotated so the anchor may be hawsed.
following sea. A sea running in the same direction as the ship's course.
foot. The lower edge of a sail.
footropes. Ropes that hang below a yard to provide footing for cadets to climb out on a yard and handle sail.
freeing ports. Openings in the side of a ship to carry off seawater that has come over the rail.
full and by. Sailing as close to the wind as possible with all sails drawing full and course changes being made to adjust for wind shifts. Sailing *full and by* allows the vessel to make as much ground to weather as possible without pinching. With all sails set, *Eagle* can sail about 75 degrees off the true wind when sailing *full and by*.
furl. To take in a sail and secure it.
futtock shrouds. Steel rods leading from the futtock band below the tops to the edge of the tops, providing a foundation for the topmast shrouds.

gaff. A spar on the mizzen used for extending the head of the spanker.
gantline. A whip (purchase) rigged aloft for general utility purposes.
gasket. Line or canvas strap used to secure a sail when furled.
goosewing. To set only the leeward side of a sail. Chafing gear may be passed around the sail at the center of the yard and the weather side remains in its gear. The mainsail may be goosewinged to prevent blanketing the foresail and the main topmast staysail when sailing with the wind abaft the beam.
gripe. Fastenings for securing a ship's boat in its cradle or to the rail.

halyard. Line used for hoisting and lowering sails and yards.
"Hand over hand." To haul on a line using one hand then the other, never losing contact or control of the line.
"Handsomely." To execute a command deliberately and carefully but not necessarily slowly.
hank. Circular metal fitting that rides on a stay and to which the luff of a staysail is seized.
haul. 1. In the Northern Hemisphere, a shift in the wind in a clockwise direction. Same as *veer*. 2. To pull without the aid of machinery.
hawsepipes. Heavy castings through which anchor chain runs from the wildcat through the deck to the anchor.
head. The top edge of a square sail that is bent to the yard. On a fore-and-aft sail, the halyard is secured to the head.

header. A temporary shift in wind direction requiring a vessel to fall off.
"Heave around." To haul on a line with the aid of machinery such as a capstan or winch.
heave to (under sail). To stop the ship's headway by turning into the wind or by backing the sails on one or more masts.
heavy weather bill. A procedure that readies the ship for riding out a storm. The bill requires rigging lifelines, lashing down loose gear, and setting maximum conditions of material and engineering readiness.
helm indicator. A dial located on the helm stand that indicates how many degrees the helm has been turned. The rudder angle indicator, located on the stack, shows how many degrees the rudder has actually moved.
"Helm's alee." Informational command to indicate that a tacking maneuver has begun.
"Hold." Do not allow the line to be eased; hold until the line parts.
house. To lower the fore and main topgallant masts so that the *Eagle* may pass safely under a bridge. The topgallant masts can be lowered approximately fifteen feet.

in irons. A vessel is *in irons* when it stops during a tack with the wind dead ahead and cannot be turned either way.
in its gear. When a sail has been taken in and is being held by its gear: buntlines, leechlines, buntleechlines, and clewlines all two-blocked and belayed.
in its lifts. A yard is *in its lifts* when the halyard

has been eased and the yard hauled down so that its entire weight is supported by the fixed lifts.
Irish pennant. Any piece of loose line or gear adrift in the rigging.

jackstay. A metal rod to which sails or lines are secured, located on top of a yard on the forward side.
jibe. A maneuver for a sailing vessel to change tacks by bringing the stern through the wind. Fore-and-aft-rigged vessels *jibe* whereas square-riggers *wear,* which is another term for a controlled jibe.
jigger. A purchase generally used to take additional strain on running rigging.

knightshead. See **dograil.**
knockdown. Sudden and extreme heeling because of a strong gust of wind.

lanyard. Any piece of small, strong line used to secure accessories to one's person while going aloft.
leather. A short strip of leather tucked into the braces after they have stretched out to mark where the yards are braced square or sharp.
lee. Away from the direction of the wind. Objects on that side are said to be to *leeward.*
lee helm. A condition where there is too much force from the sails forward of the pivot point causing the ship to fall off the wind, which must be corrected for by turning the rudder to weather to steer a straight course.
leech. The after edge of a fore-and-aft sail or the sides of a square sail.
leechlines. Lines leading to the leeches of a

square sail that haul them up to the yards for furling.

leeway. Drift of a vessel or other floating object to *leeward* (downwind).

leeward. Direction away from the wind (downwind).

"Let go and haul." Brace the yards of the foremast to the opposite tack when maneuvering under sail.

lift. 1. A lesser degree of luffing on the square sails, when the wind is almost parallel to the yards, striking along the leeches, causing them to shiver rather than fill. 2. A temporary shift in the wind allowing the vessel to turn toward the direction of the wind.

lifts. Fixed lifts are rigged on the royal, topgallant, and upper topsail yards to keep them secure when fully lowered. Movable lifts are rigged on the fore and main yards to permit moving yards in a vertical plane as required.

line. In general, sailors refer to fiber rope as line; wire rope is referred to as rope, wire rope, or just wire.

"Lively." Execute your last command quickly, either easing or hauling at a faster pace.

lizard. A short length of line having a thimble (or thimbles) spliced into its ends. Used as a leader for rigging.

luff. 1. The leading edge of a fore-and-aft sail. 2. The shake or slat of a sail when the sheet is too slack or the vessel is too close to the wind.

"Mainsail haul." Bracing the yards of the mainmast to the opposite tack when maneuvering under sail.

"Man." Station a sufficient number of cadets to handle a line considering its purpose and weather conditions.
manned and ready. A line is *manned and ready* when there are enough people to work the line properly and enough turns have been cleared off the pin so the line may be worked.
marry. To twist together two or more lines so that the friction between them will prevent the lines from running free. Lines are married to allow them to be belayed safely when a stopper is not being used.
martingale stay. The stay that runs from the dolphin striker to the stem of the ship. Provides support for the dolphin striker and bowsprit.
masthead. The top of a lower mast where the foretop or maintop is situated.
miter seam. The seam of a headsail or staysail that leads from the clew to the luff.
monkey rails. Two rails on the fo'c'sle used to belay the headsail sheets to.

off the wind. When the ship is not sailing close-hauled and the true wind is abaft the beam.
on the wind. Close-hauled, or sailing as close to the wind as possible. *Eagle* can sail approximately 75 to 80 degrees from the true wind.
outhaul. Line used to haul out the head or the foot of the spanker.
"Overhaul." Assist in rendering free. Applies to extending a tackle, hauling slack in buntlines, leechlines, and so on.

padeye. Steel ring welded to a deck or bulkhead to which gear is rigged.

pinch. To sail a ship or boat too close to the wind so that the sails lose their maximum driving power causing the vessel to slow or stall. A vessel can be *pinching* without the sails luffing.
point. One of thiry-two divisions of a compass card. One point corresponds to 11.25 degrees. *Pointing* can refer to a sailing vessel's course and ability to steer close to the wind.
pooped. A vessel is *pooped* when a heavy sea breaks over the stern or quarter. Usually occurs when running before the wind in a gale.
preventer. A line or tackle used to provide extra safety. The most common preventer on the *Eagle* is used to prevent the spanker boom from jibing.
purchase. A general term for a mechanical arrangement of blocks and line for multiplying force, often classified by its mechanical advantage. A *two-fold purchase,* two double blocks and four falls (lines between blocks), has a four-to-one advantage. *A three-fold purchase* (two treble blocks and six falls) has a six-to-one advantage.

quarter. A position 45 degrees abaft either beam; directly between *abeam* and *astern.*

ratlines. Lines seized to the shrouds upon which cadets climb to lay aloft.
rattail jigger. A light purchase with a stopper shackled to the becket of a block. Used to sweat down lines by passing the stopper around the line and hauling it down to deck.
reach. The points of sail when a sailing vessel is neither beating to windward nor running before the wind.

relative wind. The wind *Eagle*'s anemometer indicates is the combination of the true wind and the variation to it caused by the vessel's motion through the water. The wind that is felt by an observer on board a moving vessel, measured in degrees relative.

"Rise tacks and sheets." Clew up the mainsail when maneuvering under sail. A command also used to mean douse the staysails in a tack.

roband. Short length of marline used to secure the head of a square sail to the jackstay or the luff of a headsail to the hanks.

rope. In the maritime services, *rope* is wire cordage. If made of fiber, it is referred to as *line*.

rotten stuff. Any of a variety of small yarns, usually salvaged from old lines, used to stop off gear. Rotten stuff must be strong enough to hold the gear but light enough to break easily when tugged.

"Round in." Bring the blocks of a tackle together by hauling on the line.

running rigging. Movable lines and blocks used for handling sails, yards, and so on.

safety stay. The aftermost of the two jackstays on each yard. It is so called because it provides a hand hold (and a point of attachment for safety belt hooks) for personnel working on the yards.

scallops. Slack sections of the luff of a fore-and-aft sail caused by not properly hauling on the halyard when setting the sail. Scallops create turbulence and should be removed.

scotchman. Wooden battens fastened to the standing rigging to prevent chafing.

scud. To run before the wind in heavy weather with reduced sail, such as the main lower topsail and the foresail.
scupper. A drain in the deck to carry off the accumulation of rain or seawater from the waterways.
sea painter. Line used to make fast a boat's bow to a ship.
seize. To fasten ropes together by turns of small stuff.
shaft alley. The compartment aft of the engine room through which the propeller shaft runs.
sheet. Running rigging secured to the clew of a sail (opposing the clewline).
"Sheet home." When setting square sails, ease the clewlines, buntlines, and leechlines, and haul on the sheets until only a few links of the sheet chain remain above the sheet block. This command is also given to personnel on headsails and staysails to haul the sheet in and trim it to best advantage.
ship. A three or more masted sailing vessel square-rigged on all masts. (*Eagle* is technically not a ship. See **barque**.)
shoe. A fitting at the center of the upper three yards that rides in a track bolted to the mast and secures the yard to the mast.
shrouds. Standing rigging used to support a mast laterally, led athwartships from aloft to the deck.
"Slack." Pay out fairly rapidly; remove all of the strain from the line.
slatting about. Moving uncontrollably as sheets, yards, or blocks may do in a sailing evolution if not watched closely.
slot. The space between two headsails or stay-

sails. The width of the slot should be adjusted by use of the sheets to create the fastest airflow, which will then increase the driving power of the sails.

small stuff. Small cordage designated by the number of threads or by special names such as marline.

spider band. A metal band just above the deck on each mast, with fittings on which miscellaneous gear can be stowed.

spreader. Extension projecting horizontally at the crosstrees to spread backstays.

stacked. The yards are stacked when each is parallel to and aligned with the yard immediately below it.

standing part. The fixed part of any piece of running rigging; the end that is permanently secured.

stays. 1. The standing rigging that is the fore-and-aft support for the masts; some stays carry staysails. 2. An alternate term for tacking. The ship is in stays while coming through the wind and misses stays when she does not make it through the wind.

step. Masts are stepped on (rest on) secure foundations on the keel or the lower decks. The topgallant masts must be *stepped* (raised) after they have been *housed* (lowered) to go under a bridge.

stirrups. Wire rope pendants that are seized to the jackstays and are used to support the footropes.

stopper. A short length of line fixed to the deck, used to hold a line under strain while it is being belayed.

strop. A rope spliced into a circle for use around the shell of a block or bull's eye (as in a lizard).

tabling. A broad hem of extra canvas or dacron sewn into the edges of sails to reinforce them. Same as the boltrope used on older sails.
tack. 1. Lines leading forward from the clew of the courses. 2. The lower forward corner of a fore-and-aft sail.
tacking. A sailing maneuver: the process of bringing the ship's bow through the wind to get the wind on the opposite side.
tack-jigger. A tackle used to haul down the weather tack of the foresail or mainsail.
telltale. Any flag or pennant that gives an indication of the relative wind.
"Tend." Stationing one cadet, or at most two, for the purpose of easing or keeping the slack out of a line.
"That's well." Command used to indicate that a line has been hauled enough. A milder form of the command **"Avast."**
"Throw off." Take a line off the pin and see that the line runs freely. This command never applies to lines under a heavy strain, except in emergencies.
timenoguy. Lines used to support a long and heavy line such as the main braces on *Eagle*. The *timenoguy* prevents the main braces from fouling on the small boat davits when bracing around.
top. 1. Platform at the top of a mast, as foretop or maintop, though not the actual uppermost point. 2. To haul on a topping lift to hoist either the cargo or spanker boom.
top-hamper. The collective term for all yards, rigging, and gear above the deck that resist the wind.
topping lift. Purchase used for raising or taking the weight of a boom.

trick wheel. The emergency helm located on the fantail of *Eagle*.
"Trim." To adjust sails to take best advantage of the wind. Sheets, braces, and lifts are the lines normally adjusted when *trimming* sail.
truck. The top of a vessel's mast, as in the *main truck*.
truss. A heavy swivel with a horizontal and vertical pivot forming the center of motion for bracing a yard.
two-blocked. A purchase is *two-blocked* when the two blocks have been pulled as close together as possible.
tye. Part of the purchase used to raise the movable yards. On *Eagle* it consists of a chain made fast to the center of the yard. The chain is led up through a sheave in the mast down to a fly block through which the halyard purchase is rove.

unfurl. To cast loose a sail by throwing off the gaskets.
"Up behind." Used when belaying a line and enough turns are on the pin so that one person can hold it. A command to those behind the line captain to drop the line so that the line may be belayed quickly.

vang. A line leading from the mizzen gaff to the deck to keep it steady when the spanker is not set (used in pairs on *Eagle*).
veer. 1. In the Northern Hemisphere, a shift in the direction of the wind in a clockwise direction. See also **haul.** 2. To pay out or let out a greater

length of chain or rope; specifically, to *veer* chain when anchoring.

waist. The portion of the main weather deck between the raised fo'c'sle deck and the poop deck.
"Walk away with." To grasp a line with both hands and *walk away* (move away) with it. Used when hauling on a line, usually a halyard.
waterway. The gutter at the sides of a ship's deck to carry excess water to the scuppers.
wearing. The process of bringing the ship's stern through the wind to get the wind on the opposite side; same as jibing on a fore-and-aft rigged vessel.
weather. On the side toward the wind. Objects on that side are referred to as *to windward* or *to weather.*
weather helm. A condition where lee rudder must be used in order to keep the vessel on a steady course. This is caused by more force aft of the pivot point forcing the bow to windward. Although excessive weather helm is undesirable, *Eagle* and most sailing vessels are designed to sail with some weather helm, especially when sailing *on the wind* (usually less than 10 degrees of rudder).
worm, parcel, and serve. A method of protecting standing rigging. Worming is the process of filling the lays of a rope with small stuff wound spirally. Parceling consists of winding tarred canvas around a rope, while serving is winding small stuff tightly around a rope to hold the worming and parceling in position.

yard. A spar rigged horizontally on a mast, to which the head of a square sail is bent (made fast).

yardarm. Outboard end of a yard.

yoke. The U-shaped steel bar that is secured to the center of the yard and to the truss.

Index

The Naval Institute Press is the book-publishing arm of the U.S. Naval Institute, a private, nonprofit, membership society for sea service professionals and others who share an interest in naval and maritime affairs. Established in 1873 at the U.S. Naval Academy in Annapolis, Maryland, where its offices remain today, the Naval Institute has members worldwide.

Members of the Naval Institute support the education programs of the society and receive the influential monthly magazine *Proceedings* and discounts on fine nautical prints and on ship and aircraft photos. They also have access to the transcripts of the Institute's Oral History Program and get discounted admission to any of the Institute-sponsored seminars offered around the country.

The Naval Institute also publishes *Naval History* magazine. This colorful bimonthly is filled with entertaining and thought-provoking articles, first-person reminiscences, and dramatic art and photography. Members receive a discount on *Naval History* subscriptions.

The Naval Institute's book-publishing program, begun in 1898 with basic guides to naval practices, has broadened its scope in recent years to include books of more general interest. Now the Naval Institute Press publishes about one hundred titles each year, ranging from how-to books on boating and navigation to battle histories, biographies, ship and aircraft guides, and novels. Institute members receive discounts of 20 to 50 percent on the Press's more than eight hundred books in print.

Full-time students are eligible for special half-price membership rates. Life memberships are also available.

For a free catalog describing Naval Institute Press books currently available, and for further information about subscribing to *Naval History* magazine or about joining the U.S. Naval Institute, please write to: